DOES GOD BELONG IN THE BEDROOM?

DOES
GOD
BELONG IN THE
BEDROOM ?

BY RABBI MICHAEL GOLD

The Jewish Publication Society

Philadelphia   Jerusalem

5753·1992

Library of Congress Cataloging-in-Publication Data

Gold, Michael, 1950–
    Does God belong in the bedroom? / by Michael Gold.—1st ed.
    p.   cm.
    Includes bibliographical references (p.   ) and index.
    ISBN 0–8276–0421–1
    1. Sex—Religious aspects—Judaism.   2. Judaism—Doctrines.
I. Title.
BM720.S4G65   1992
296.3'8566—dc20   92–11984
                                                              CIP
                                                               AC

Designed by Denise Avayou

For JEFFREY GOLD

May his memory be for a blessing

CONTENTS

10. IMPLICATIONS BEYOND THE BEDROOM   181

PREFACE

We live in an age of sexual confusion. The values of the past no longer seem quite adequate for our needs; we feel compelled to seek standards and guidance, to know right from wrong.

In my years as a congregational rabbi, I have been involved in a search for values. My previous book, *And Hannah Wept: Infertility, Adoption, and the Jewish Couple* (Philadelphia: The Jewish Publication Society, 1988) presents a Jewish perspective on infertility and adoption, an area in which I gained expertise from personal experience. Sexuality, I have discovered, is an even more challenging topic.

Traditional Jewish sources clearly defined when sex was permissible and what kind of sexual behavior was allowed. The rabbis taught that sex belongs within marriage. To prevent temptation, the intermingling of the sexes was kept to a minimum. In talmudic times marriages were arranged at a very young age: eighteen for a boy and as young as twelve and a half for a girl. For both boys and girls, even younger marriages were permissible and recommended by many authorities.

Outside of marriage, all sexual activity was proscribed. Even masturbation was forbidden, and homosexuality was considered an abomination. To protect family life, adultery and incest were absolute taboos; in the Torah they are punishable by death.

Even within marriage, traditional Judaism demanded sexual discipline. The laws of family purity ensured that a husband and wife slept separately and avoided any physical contact during part of each month. Birth control was frowned upon although permitted under certain circumstances. Large families were the norm, and a family without many children, particularly without sons, was to be pitied.

In traditional Jewish society, the roles of men and women were clearly defined. There were clear standards of modesty. Improper sexual behavior and immodest conduct were *ḥukkat hagoyim*, "the way of the gentiles." Jews simply did not behave in those ways.

Throughout history many Jews did not live up to the standards as articulated in the traditional Jewish codes, but even the Jew who fell short knew what the community standards were. Jews knew that promiscuity, adultery, incest, homosexuality, and immodesty were wrong and that marriage and family were the ideal.

During the past several decades, the traditional standards that developed over millennia have broken down. Among the many factors contributing to this breakdown are later marriage, the invention of oral contraceptives and other effective birth control methods, the rise of the feminist movement, the legalization of abortion, the acceptance of divorce, the push for gay rights, the secularization of society, and, perhaps most important, the dissolution of traditional family life. The old rules, developed in simpler times, no longer work for the vast majority of modern Jews. The question is, how do we develop new rules?

Before I begin to explore Jewish sexual ethics, a personal note is in order. I grew up in the sixties, a decade that witnessed the greatest challenge ever to the traditional standards of sexual behavior. Although I may have been a bit more conservative than many of my contemporaries, the touchstone for my morality and behavior during my early adult years was the ethics of the free love generation.

In the seventies I began my discovery of traditional Jewish law and values. My commitment to Jewish observance came slowly as

I grappled with the dietary laws, the Sabbath, and the discipline of daily prayer. After careful soul searching, I decided to pursue a career in the rabbinate. I saw the role of rabbi as a bridge between Jews and Judaism. Being a rabbi meant seriously studying the tradition and interpreting it to Jews as they live today. Occasionally it meant rethinking and adjusting the tradition so that it became viable for modern Jews. Equally often, it meant encouraging modern Jews to integrate creatively traditional values and practices into their daily lives.

I have always believed that the ideal rabbi ought to combine the qualities of the brothers Moses and Aaron. Moses, according to the Talmud, used to say: "Let the law split the mountain."[1] In other words, the law should be applied with full rigor, with no room for compromise or compassion. Moses had little patience for the human weaknesses of the people he tried to lead through the wilderness for forty years. Aaron, on the other hand, was known as a lover of peace and a pursuer of peace, qualities that made him tolerate, even participate in, the sin of the Golden Calf. Aaron failed to realize that there are times the law cannot be compromised. My approach to the rabbinate has been to find a balance between the rigor of Moses and the compassion of Aaron.

Sexual ethics presents a particularly difficult challenge for a rabbi with this pragmatic philosophy. The Talmud teaches, "Go out and see what the people are doing."[2] But suppose that what the people are doing is far from the tradition as developed in the Talmud and codes. Is it possible to bridge the gap?

Today many Jews remain unmarried, often through their twenties and thirties and sometimes forever. The Jewish divorce rate has risen dramatically, and many adults are widowed at an age when they are still sexually active. A high percentage of adults have no marriage partner through much of their adulthood. Is it realistic for them to remain celibate?

As a rabbi, I must deal with real situations. When I meet with a bride and groom before their wedding, how do I ask for their address and telephone number? More often than not they are already living together, but they are embarrassed to share that with me, their rabbi. Or, perhaps worse, they are not embarrassed; living together has become the norm rather than the exception.

If they are living together, what do I write in the *ketubbah*, the traditional marriage document? The classical wording uses the term *betultah*, or "virgin," for a woman who has never been married. The financial terms of the ketubbah also depend on the bride's virginal status. As a rabbi, do I write a falsehood in the ketubbah to protect the bride's reputation in public, or do I tell the truth, assuming that nobody cares and that premarital virginity is a thing of the past? Or should the traditional *ketubbah* be rewritten altogether?

I once performed the wedding of a couple who had been living together for about a year. The bride's parents refused to pay for or participate in the wedding. They told me, "Why do they need a wedding? They're living together anyway." What do I say to these parents? For that matter, what do I say to a couple living together unmarried who want to join my synagogue as a family? Does the congregation accept them, and would that acceptance put a stamp of approval on nonmarital sexual relations?

The issues of nonmarital sex become particularly difficult when I deal with the teens in my youth group. Many teens today are sexually active, often at a very young age. Recently I was asked by the local public high school to offer a Jewish perspective on a proposal for an on-campus clinic that would dispense birth control pills. What guidance can Jewish tradition provide for such a proposal? How do we teach sexual morality to our youth if we tolerate promiscuity in our adults? On a youth group retreat, do we allow boys and girls to bring sleeping bags and share one big room, or do we insist that they sleep separately? What can we do as a community about the appalling rate of teen pregnancy?

Adultery is also no longer a simple matter of black or white. A woman whose husband had carried on a series of affairs once wanted my advice on whether to take him back. How do I reconcile my belief in the importance of marital fidelity with my belief that a marriage always ought to be saved? Also, how do I explain to modern Jews certain difficult traditional laws regarding adultery? For example, according to halakhah, a woman who commits adultery is forever forbidden to her husband. Similarly, a child born from adultery is forever tainted as a *mamzer* and cannot marry a Jew of legitimate birth. What about the case in which one marital partner is incapacitated and the other partner wants neither divorce nor a life of celibacy?

The gay rights movement has also raised numerous difficult questions. I was recently called by my local city council to testify on a gay rights bill. How can I reconcile the Jewish commitment to equal rights with the clear prohibition in the Torah against homosexuality? How should Jews react to gay synagogues that have formed in most major metropolitan centers? This question is particularly painful because the history of gay persecution parallels that of Jewish persecution. Both Jews and gays were victims of the Nazi Holocaust, and even today gays encounter the same kind of bigotry that was once the norm against Jews.

I have confronted the issue of homosexuality a number of times as a rabbi. Once an observant Jew who was gay came to me for counseling after breaking up with his gay lover. Should he be encouraged to pursue another relationship? How can I as a rabbi help him without compromising Judaic principles? AIDS, although not necessarily a gay disease, has certainly influenced how we view the gay community. What responsibility does Judaism owe persons with AIDS? Can we say that a disease has a moral cause?

Even within marriage issues regarding sexuality arise. As I mentioned above, I have come slowly to a life of religious observance after much study and careful thought. How do my wife and I integrate the Jewish stance toward sexuality into our marriage? Is there room for variety and experimentation? Are the traditional laws of family purity still applicable? Are we permitted to use birth control?

In our particular case, the problem was not preventing pregnancy but achieving it. Today new reproductive techniques can help infertile couples have children. Many religious leaders, particularly in the Catholic Church and among fundamentalist Protestants, have attacked these methods as separating the creation of children from the sexual act. Does Jewish tradition condone such techniques?

Other questions arise after children are born. How do we inculcate in our children proper sexual values? How do we instill both a comfort with their own bodies and an appropriate sense of modesty? Do we condone masturbation? How do we educate our children about sex? Should my synagogue or the Jewish day school sponsor a sex education program for its youngsters?

As a rabbi, I have grappled with all these questions. The purpose of this book is to suggest answers appropriate for our time. It is written for serious Jews, regardless of denomination or affiliation. It will draw from the wells of Jewish tradition to seek guidance for today's society. It will explore what biblical and rabbinic sources teach about human sexuality; marital, nonmarital, and extramarital sex; modesty; homosexuality; birth control; abortion; the new reproductive techniques; and sex education.

Let me share a thought about my particular approach. Judaism contains a vast reservoir of rabbinic sources on sexuality, ranging from extreme asceticism to a frank celebration of the sexual drive. Any study of Jewish sources will naturally be selective. Without ignoring the negatives within our tradition, I have tried to emphasize sources that see our sexual drive as God's gift, to be used to achieve both happiness and holiness. I believe this approach is authentic and will have the greatest meaning for modern Jews.

My goal in this book is to apply traditional teachings to life as it is lived today. The results may not necessarily conform to traditional codifications of Jewish law, but they should demonstrate that Judaism has much to teach us about one of our most powerful drives and most fundamental human activities.

The insights of many people were invaluable in preparing this book. A variety of scholars and rabbis have spoken and written on issues related to sexuality; since it is a mitzvah to quote a teaching *be-shem omro* (in the name of its author), I refer to these teachers throughout the book.

Dr. Ronald Brauner first invited me to teach a course in Jewish sexual ethics for the Hebrew Institute of Pittsburgh, forcing me to apply Jewish law systematically to American reality. I continued to teach this course at Beth El Congregation and the Jewish Community Center of Pittsburgh. I also began to lecture on sexual ethics in numerous cities around the country. It was often my students who gave me my greatest insights.

Sheila Segal, former editor-in-chief of the Jewish Publication Society, encouraged me to write this book and helped me with its overall organization. The current editor-in-chief, Ellen Frankel, went over the manuscript line by line, always looking for ways to improve the work. Her vast knowledge of Judaism and her ear for the English language were extremely valuable in shaping this book.

I want to give a special thank-you to my wife, Evelyn, for her encouragement, insights, patience, and love. She is my partner in trying to build a contemporary Jewish life that still draws deeply from the wells of tradition.

Finally, I want to dedicate this book to the memory of my brother Jeffrey, a victim of AIDS. Jeffrey would probably disagree

with many of my conclusions in this book, but our long discussions about sexuality and spirituality helped sharpen my thinking
and make me more sensitive to those with a different sexual orientation. If one victim of AIDS receives more compassionate treatment as a result of this book, it will be a fitting tribute to his
memory.

DOES GOD BELONG IN THE BEDROOM?

1

God in the Bedroom

You shall serve God with both your inclinations.
Rashi on Deuteronomy 6:5

THIS BOOK begins with a premise: there is a Jewish way to regard sex and a Jewish way to have sex.

This statement may surprise most modern Jews, many of whom feel that religion ought to be concerned with more lofty matters—God, life and death, sin and redemption. Others say that religion ought to be concerned with day-to-day spiritual matters such as prayer and the liturgical calendar; still others, that religion ought to be concerned with the practical questions of building a better world, matters of ethics and social action. Sex, they believe, is too private and too physical to be the concern of religion. Once when I was invited to speak on sexual ethics, I was told, "Rabbi, religion belongs in the synagogue or church, but please keep it out of the bedroom."

This attitude is not authentically Jewish; it reflects the biases of Western culture, which were greatly influenced by the ancient Greeks. The Greek philosopher Plato spoke of the separation between forms and ideals, between body and spirit, with the greatest emphasis on matters of the spirit. This approach was quite influential in early Christian thought and subsequently in Western culture. From this premise emerged the notion that religion should be concerned primarily with matters of the spirit and that such physical functions as sex or, for that matter, eating and drinking are secondary religious concerns.

Judaism has a different approach. The Talmud provides us with a fascinating story illustrating the Jewish view:

> R. Kahana once went in and hid under Rab's bed. He heard him chatting [with his wife] and joking and doing what he required. He said to him: "One would think that Abba's never sipped the dish before." He said to him: "Kahana, are you here? Go out, because it is rude." He replied: "It is a matter of Torah, and I need to learn."[1]

The story of a student hiding under his rabbi's bed while the rabbi makes love to his wife obviously does not negate the traditional Jewish concern with modesty. It does provide a penetrating insight into the Jewish view that the sexual behavior of a great sage with his wife is also Torah.

Indeed, Judaism is concerned with every area of human endeavor. Based on a verse in Psalms, "All my bones shall say 'Lord, who is like You?'" (Ps. 35:10), the rabbis taught that we are to serve God with all our limbs. Jewish law is not concerned simply with how we pray or how we treat our fellow but also with how we work, dress, eat, drink, and have sex.

Let us explore some basic Jewish teachings about sex that form the foundation for the rest of the book.

SEX, LIKE ALL OF GOD'S CREATION, IS GOOD

The Torah never explicitly lays out a sexual ethic; rather, it hints at certain attitudes in numerous passages. These attitudes are further explored in the rabbinic interpretations of these passages articulated in the Talmud and the midrash.

The Torah sees the world and everything in it as essentially good: "And God saw all that He made, and found it very good" (Gen. 1:30). This goodness includes sexual activity. After creating human beings, God blesses them and tells them, "Be fertile and increase, fill the earth and master it" (Gen. 1:28). Thus sexual activity is a basic part of God's creation; as such it must be good.

For the most part, Judaism rejected the negative teachings about sex that later became prevalent in Christianity. In fact, the rabbis throughout the talmudic period and the Middle Ages often spoke of sexual relations as a wonderful part of God's creation. One famous passage teaches:

> We the possessors of the Holy Torah believe that God, may He be praised, created all, as His wisdom decreed, and did not create anything ugly or shameful. For if sexual intercourse were repulsive, then the reproductive organs are also repulsive. . . . If the reproductive organs are repulsive, how did the Creator fashion something blemished? If that were so, we should find that His deeds were not perfect. . . .[2]

Sexual relations, *at the proper time and in the proper context*, are part of God's plan and are essentially good.

In the Torah, human beings are portrayed as sexual creatures. When God creates Adam, God's immediate response is that Adam has no fitting helper—that is, no sexual partner. Adam gives names to all the various animals, but none is found to be a fitting partner for him:

> So the LORD God cast a deep sleep upon the man; and, while he slept, He took one of his ribs and closed up the flesh at that spot. And the LORD God fashioned the rib that He had taken from the man into a woman; and He brought her to the man. Then the man said, "This one at last is bone of my bones and flesh of my flesh. This one shall be called Woman, for from man was she taken." Hence a man leaves his father and mother and clings to his wife, so that they become one flesh. (Gen. 2:21–24)

The creation stories in the Torah suggest two purposes of sexual activity. The first and most obvious is *procreation*. Sex is part of God's plan for populating the world; it fulfills God's will for both animals and humans. The rabbis used the words of Isaiah as a proof text: "The Creator of heaven who alone is God. Who formed the earth and made it, Who alone established it. He did not create it a waste, but formed it for habitation" (Isa. 45:18).[3]

The second purpose of sexual relations is *companionship*, which the Torah seems to regard as an even greater justification for sexual relations than procreation. In Jewish tradition, the belief that "it is not good for man to be alone" is as important if not more important than the command to "be fruitful and increase." The Torah uses the term *yada*—"to know"—to indicate a sexual relationship. Sex is thus considered more than a mere biological act; it involves intimate knowledge shared by two human beings.

The positive attitude of Judaism toward sexuality stands in sharp contrast with a more negative picture that developed in early Christianity. Although Christians disagreed on the nature of Adam's sin in the Bible, it was generally believed to be tied up with sexuality. Paul, the founder of Christianity, particularly emphasized this attitude. According to Elaine Pagels, a Christian scholar:

> He [Paul] often speaks of marriage in negative terms, as a sop for those too weak to do what is best: renounce sexual activity altogether. Paul admits that marriage is "not sin" yet argues that it makes both partners slaves to each other's sexual needs and desires, no longer free to devote their energies "to the Lord" [1 Cor. 7:1–35].[4]

Admittedly, Paul was speaking to a community that believed the kingdom of God was imminent. Even after such hopes failed, however, this identification of sex with sin was further developed by the early fathers of the church, particularly Augustine, and has remained influential in Christianity to this day.

THE POTENTIAL FOR MISUSE OF THE SEXUAL DRIVE

Even though the Torah finds sex essentially good, it does recognize the potential for misuse. The early stories of Genesis cite numerous examples of improper sexual behavior. For example, ten generations after the creation of Adam, the Torah speaks of the sexual degeneration of both humans and animals. In response, God brings a flood upon the world and destroys almost all of His creation. Only Noah and his family are saved. The Torah justifies God's action: "The earth became corrupt before God; the earth was filled with lawlessness. . . . God saw how corrupt the earth was, for all flesh had corrupted its ways on earth" (Gen. 6:11–12). The rabbis understood the word "corrupt" to mean forbidden sexual relations, *davar ervah*.[5] Rashi comments that "even cattle, beasts, and birds were coupling with those not of their species."[6]

Even though Noah is saved from the flood and given a chance to start life anew, one of his first acts involves improper sexual activity. He plants a vineyard, makes wine, and falls into a drunken stupor in his tent. Ham, his middle son, sees his father's nakedness and tells his two brothers. Later Noah awakes, realizes what his son has done, and curses him. The Torah speaks in euphemisms but seems to indicate an incestuous-homosexual incident. The story clearly suggests that something immoral has happened and that certain sexual activities are against God's plan.

Other Torah sources give examples of improper sexual behavior. Lot's daughters have an incestuous relationship with their father (Gen. 19:30–37). The sons of Jacob take revenge on Shekhem and the people of his city after their sister is raped (Gen. 34). The wife of Potiphar tries to seduce Joseph into an adulterous relationship (Gen. 39:7–12). The people of Egypt and Canaan are seen as an evil influence because of their sexual activities (Lev.

18:1–4). Prostitution, common in the ancient Near East, is forbidden in the holy Temple (Deut. 23:18–19).

Thus the Torah sees sexual activities as essentially good but as carrying great potential for misuse. It recognizes that the human sexual drive is great and that often resistance to improper sex is not easy. For this reason, the rabbis identified the sexual drive with the *yetzer hara*, the evil inclination.

SEX AND THE EVIL INCLINATION

According to rabbinic tradition, every human being is born with both an inclination to do good, *yetzer hatov*, and an inclination to do evil, *yetzer hara*.[7] The *yetzer hara* corresponds to a person's untamed urges and appetites, particularly the sexual drive. The biblical source of the evil inclination is God's promise to Noah never again to destroy the earth since "the devisings of man's mind are evil from his youth" (Gen. 8:21).

The rabbis also recognized that the *yetzer hara* is not entirely evil but has a vital role to play in human life. One famous midrash states, "Were it not for the *yetzer hara*, no man would build a house, marry a wife, or beget children."[8] A rabbinic tale stresses the importance of the evil inclination:

> [The people Israel] said, "Since this is a time of grace for us, let us pray that the yetzer hara be handed over to us."
> They prayed and he was given to them.
> But the prophet Elijah warned them: "Understand, that if you kill the yetzer hara, the whole world will collapse."
> Nevertheless, they imprisoned the yetzer hara for three days. But when they looked for a fresh egg, none could be found in all of the land of Israel.
> "What shall we do?" the people asked one another. "Shall we kill him? But without the yetzer hara the world cannot survive."
> . . . So they blinded him and let him go (thus limiting its power).[9]

Jewish tradition recognizes the importance of the sexual drive in human beings. The key is to keep the urge under control and channel it to serve God. Jews should thus serve God with both their inclinations.

The presence of a powerful *yetzer hara* does not mean that a person is evil. On the contrary, the rabbis recognized that sometimes the more pious the person, the more powerful the *yetzer hara*. This notion is illustrated in a famous talmudic story about the great sage Abaye:

> Abaye heard a certain man saying to a woman, "Let us arise and go on our way." Abaye said, "I will follow them in order to keep them away from transgression," and so he followed them for three parasangs across the meadows. When they parted company, he heard them say, "Your company is pleasant, the way is long." Abaye said, "If it had been I, I could not have restrained myself," and so he went and leaned in deep anguish against a doorpost, when a certain old man came up to him and taught him: the greater the man, the greater is his yetzer hara.[10]

Judaism has long recognized that a great man can be driven by a powerful sexual drive. Perhaps that idea can explain the fall of so many political and religious leaders to sexual indiscretions in recent years.

According to Jewish tradition, the man with the strongest *yetzer hara* was King David—the very man with whom God made a special covenant and whom God designated as the progenitor of the messiah. In a midrash, the rabbis explained how David yielded to temptation and lusted after Batsheva, committing first adultery and then murder:

> Rav Judah said in Rav's name: One should never (intentionally) bring himself to the test, since David king of Israel did so and fell. He said unto Him: "Sovereign of the Universe. Why do we say in the daily Amida 'the God of Abraham, the God of Isaac, and the God of Jacob'

but not 'the God of David'?" He replied, "They were tried by me, but you were not." Then he replied, "Examine me, O Lord, and try me." He answered, "I will test thee, and yet grant thee a special privilege, for I did not inform them [of the nature of their trial beforehand], yet I inform thee that I will try thee in a matter of adultery." R. Johanan said, ". . . he forgot the halakha that there is a small organ in man which satisfies him in his hunger but makes him hunger when satisfied."[11]

The theological notion of a *yetzer hara* does not at all correspond to the Christian idea of original sin. According to Christianity, human beings are sinful in their very essence and can find salvation only by divine grace. In Judaism humans are neither inherently good nor bad; they are driven by inner forces identified as the good and evil inclinations. The *yetzer hara* only has a *potential* for evil. The object is to direct the evil inclination toward good ends, that is, the service of God. That is why Ben Zoma said, "Who is strong? He who is in control of his inclination."[12]

Judaism sees the sexual drive as basic to human beings. It is wrong to suppress it totally; therefore, there is no tradition of celibacy in Jewish writings. The goal of a Jew is to channel the sexual drive into appropriate behavior and, by doing so, to serve God.

THE JEWISH PEOPLE AND SEXUAL MORALITY

In traditional rabbinic thinking, Jewish sexual morality distinguished the Jewish people from the other nations. According to the midrash, even when the Israelites were slaves in ancient Egypt, they maintained their standards of sexual morality:

R. Huna in the name of R. Hiyya b. Abba said, Our mother Sarah went down to Egypt, and because she hedged herself against unchastity all the women were protected on her account. Joseph went down to Egypt, and because he hedged himself against unchastity Israel was protected on his account. R. Hiyya b. Abba stated: The act of hedging themselves against unchastity was in itself sufficiently meritorious to procure redemption for Israel. R. Huna stated in the name of Bar Kappara: Israel was redeemed from Egypt on account of four things, because they did not change their names, they did not change their language, they did not go tale-bearing, and none of them was found to have been sexually immoral.[13]

This midrash presents an idealized view of ancient Israel. The Torah numbers about 600,000 adult male Israelites in ancient Egypt, yet not a single one was sexually immoral!

Jewish law reflects the higher standard of sexual behavior required by the rabbis. For example, the Torah states that a Kohen (a member of the priesthood) may not marry a woman of questionable sexual morality: "They shall not marry a woman degraded by harlotry [*zonah*] nor shall they marry one divorced from her husband. For they are holy to their God" (Lev. 21:7). The term *zonah* is not defined precisely. The rabbis interpreted it to include any proselyte to Judaism.[14] In rabbinic times, non-Jews did not maintain the same standards of morality as Jews, and any proselyte woman was suspect. Among Orthodox Jews today, the prohibition against the marriage of a Kohen and a convert is still practiced; Conservative Jews permit such marriages, and Reform Jews have dropped the category of Kohen altogether.

The centrality of sexual morality to Jewish self-identity is also demonstrated by the synagogue ritual on the holiest day of the year, Yom Kippur. A special Torah reading at *minḥah* services on Yom Kippur afternoon focuses on sexual conduct. It is a particularly holy time; congregants have been fasting for nearly twenty-four hours. They have abstained from any sexual activity. Soon the closing *ne'ilah* prayer will begin, with its final plea for forgiveness. On the surface, the Torah reading at this moment seems particularly incongruous:

The Lord spoke to Moses saying: Speak to the Israelite people and say to them: I the LORD am your God. You shall not copy the practices of the land of Egypt where you dwelt, or of the land of Canaan to which I am taking you; nor shall you follow their laws. . . . None of you shall come near anyone of his own flesh to uncover nakedness: I am the LORD. (Lev. 18:1–6)

The passage is followed by a long list of forbidden sexual relationships.

The Reform movement and some Conservative congregations have been sufficiently troubled by this reading to replace it with another.[15] Traditionalists, on the other hand, argue that there is a valuable lesson in this particular reading. The purpose of Yom Kippur, they claim, is *teshuvah*, which literally means to get back on the right path. Judaism rejects the notion of original sin. *Het*, or sin, means missing the mark or straying from the path. Through a day of fasting and prayer, Jews try to redirect their lives. No area of human behavior offers more temptations to stray from the path than one's sexuality. How appropriate, therefore, to have a Torah reading on Yom Kippur afternoon regarding proper and improper sexual activity.

THOUGHTS VERSUS ACTION

In 1976, when Jimmy Carter was first running for the presidency, he created quite a stir by saying in a *Playboy* interview, "I have lusted in my heart." Here was a married man publicly admitting that he had been attracted to women besides his wife! The adverse reactions to his comments almost cost Carter the presidency.

Significantly, most Jews reacted to the Carter interview with indifference, for Judaism is primarily concerned with action as opposed to thoughts or feelings. What happens in the privacy of one's thoughts is a relatively minor concern. On the other hand, had Carter actually committed adultery, as another presidential candidate did later, Jews would have had reason to be outraged.

Here Jewish tradition differs sharply from Christianity, which puts great importance on one's inner being—what one thinks and believes. Ultimate salvation comes through personal faith. Even in our popular parlance, a "good Christian" is one who believes a certain way. In Judaism, in contrast, a person is judged not by faith but by actions. Judaism is less concerned with the state of one's inner being than with one's activity. A "good Jew" is not one who thinks a certain way but one who acts a certain way.

According to Dennis Prager and Joseph Telushkin, who have written a popular book on this theme:

> Whether or not Jesus was the Messiah is not the most important question that divides Judaism and Christianity. The major difference between Judaism and Christianity lies in the importance each religion attaches to faith and actions. In Judaism, God considers people's actions to be more important than faith; acting in accordance with biblical and rabbinic law is the Jews' central obligation. As Christianity developed, however, it did away with most of these laws, and faith became its central demand.[16]

The dichotomy between Christianity and Judaism is reflected in the realm of sexual ethics. In Christianity, one's thoughts are judged. The New Testament proclaims, "You have heard that it was said 'You shall not commit adultery,' but I say to you that every one who looks at a woman lustfully has already committed adultery with his heart" (Matt. 5:27–28). In Judaism, on the other hand, behavior, not the state of one's thoughts, is the basis of judgment. A particular sexual act may be forbidden or permitted; a particular sexual thought is not subject to legal strictures.

Two examples suffice. Judaism prohibits homosexual acts, an issue that I deal with at length in chapter 8, but it is only the acts that are forbidden, not the state of being. One may be a homosexual; one may fantasize about members of one's own sex. Until one acts on that desire, one has not broken Jewish law.

Likewise, Judaism allows freedom to fantasize. The Talmud

discusses whether it is permissible, when one is having intercourse with one's wife, to fantasize about another woman. As surprising as it may seem, the Talmud permits it. An act is judged not by what happens in one's head but by what one does with one's body.

In addition, Judaism judges acts, not people. A particular act may be considered sinful; a person may be considered a sinner while committing that act. That person, however, is not evil in his or her essence. Judaism always leaves room for *teshuvah*, an attitude best illustrated by a wonderful story involving Rabbi Meir and his wife Beruriah:

> There were once some highwaymen in the neighborhood of R. Meir who caused him a great deal of trouble. R. Meir accordingly prayed that they should die. His wife Beruriah said to him: How do you make out [that such a prayer is permitted?]. . . . Rather pray for them that they should repent, and there will be no more wicked men. He did pray for them and they repented.[17]

The Talmud gives another example closer to our theme, involving the *teshuvah* of a rabbi with an addiction for prostitutes:

> It was said of Rabbi Eleazar ben Dordia that he did not leave out any harlot in the world without coming to her. Once, on hearing that there was a certain harlot in one of the towns by the sea who accepted a purse of denarii for her hire, he took a purse of denarii and crossed seven rivers for her sake. When he was with her, she blew forth breath and said: As this blown breath will not return to its place, so will Eleazar b. Dordia never be received in repentance.
>
> He thereupon went, sat between two hills and mountains and exclaimed: O hills and mountains, plead for mercy for me. They replied, how shall we pray for you? We stand in need of it ourselves. . . . So he exclaimed: Heaven and earth, plead for mercy for me. They too replied: How shall we pray for you? We stand in need of it ourselves. . . . He then exclaimed: Sun and moon, plead for mercy for me. But they also replied: How shall we pray for you? We stand in

need of it ourselves. . . . He exclaimed: Stars and constellations, plead for mercy for me. Said they: How shall we pray for you? We stand in need of it ourselves.

Said he: The matter then depends on me alone. Having placed his head between his knees, he wept aloud until his soul departed. Then a heavenly voice was heard proclaiming: Rabbi Eleazar b. Dordia is destined for the life of the world to come.[18]

Even after the worst sexual transgressions, *teshuvah* is always possible. In keeping with this philosophy, this book will study whether particular sexual acts are permissible or impermissible, proper or improper, holy or less than holy from a Jewish perspective. It is the action that will be judged, not the person performing the act.

BEYOND GOOD TO HOLY

The rabbis discussed the permissible or forbidden nature of various types of sexual activity. Jewish mystics gave cosmic significance to the sexual act. According to them, sex, within the proper context and with proper intention, touched the very soul of the universe.

The roots of this approach lie in the Bible's highly erotic book, *Shir Ha-Shirim*, or Song of Songs. A few sample passages give the flavor of the book:

O, give me of the kisses of your mouth,
For your love is more delightful than wine. (1:2)

He brought me to the banquet room
And his banner of love was over me.
"Sustain me with raisin cakes,
Refresh me with apples,
For I am faint with love."
His left hand was under my head,
His right arm embraced me. (2:4–6)

I have come to my garden,
My own, my bride;

I have plucked my myrrh and spice,
Eaten my honey and honeycomb,
Drunk my wine and my milk.
Eat, lovers, and drink:
Drink deep of love! (5:1)

Whether such a book had a place in the sacred canon caused great controversy among the rabbis of the Talmud. Many rabbis felt that it should be excluded, but Rabbi Akiba, well known for his mystic tendencies, forcibly argued for the book's inclusion:

R. Akiba said: God forbid! No man in Israel contends that Song of Songs renders the hands unclean (belongs in the canon). The whole world is not worth the day whereon the Song of Songs was given to Israel, for all the Writings are sacred, but the Song of Songs is the most sacred of all.[19]

Rabbi Akiba saw the book as a metaphor for the relationship between God and the people Israel. Later mystics saw the relationship or covenant in blatantly sexual terms: God as the husband, Israel as His bride. Just as the relationship between God and His chosen people is holy, so the human sexual relationship has a similar potential for holiness. This metaphor is one of the reasons Judaism praises sex between husband and wife on the Sabbath evening.[20] The holiness of the Sabbath is joined to the holiness of the sexual act, adding to the holiness of the universe.

Even so, the rabbis were well aware that despite their lofty language a man and a woman may not be thinking of redeeming the universe when they fulfill their sexual needs. Their realism is clearly reflected in a midrash quoting King David on his father Jesse:

Did father Jesse really intend to bring me into the world? Why, he had only his own pleasure in mind. . . . As soon as they had satisfied their desires, he turned his face to one side and she turned her face to the other side. It was You who then led every drop [of semen] to its proper place.[21]

In reality, it is all but impossible to begin the sexual act with only holiness in mind. Accordingly, the rabbis did not ordain a blessing before the sexual act as they did before other mitzvot.

Whatever the intention, sex in the proper context and under proper circumstances does become a way of achieving holiness. The rabbis taught, "When a husband and wife unite in holiness, there the divine presence abides."[22] The mystics believed that small day-to-day acts done correctly have the potential to bring about the redemption of the universe. To the mystic mind, sex has consequences far beyond procreation or personal pleasure.

DOES GOD CARE ABOUT SEXUAL BEHAVIOR?

One of the most enlightening passages in the Torah is the story of Joseph and Potiphar's wife. Joseph, brought to Egypt to be a slave, is made the personal attendant to Potiphar, chief steward of Pharaoh. One day when Potiphar is at work, his wife tries to seduce Joseph. Joseph refuses her advances and answers:

> Look, with me here, my master gives no thought to anything in this house, and all that he owns he has placed in my hands. He wields no more authority in this house than I, and he has withheld nothing from me except yourself, since you are his wife. How then could I do this most wicked thing, *and sin before God?* (Exod. 39:8–9)

Joseph clearly understands that adultery is not simply a betrayal of trust toward his human master; it is also a sin against God. Even if Potiphar and his wife had an open marriage permitting each other different sexual partners, such sexual promiscuity would be against God's laws. This passage reinforces the notion that God cares about our sexual behavior.

In Judaism, every sexual act must be judged in terms of God's will for human beings in general and for Jews in particular. Some sexual acts are clear transgressions, hurtful to the individual and society. Other sexual acts are mitzvot, increasing the holiness of the universe. Sex has religious significance, and God *does* belong in the bedroom.

The Jewish approach is therefore quite different from modern liberal thinking. In our secular society, a particular sexual act is judged as sinful only if it is hurtful or exploitative. Any sexual encounter between consenting adults for their mutual pleasure is considered permissible. In contrast, Judaism teaches that sex has a meaning beyond the mutual pleasure of the participants. It is a spiritual as well as a physical act. God does care about what we do with our bodies. There are sexual activities which are not hurtful but which Jewish law would nevertheless forbid. Jewish laws regarding sexual behavior have a purpose beyond physical pleasure. They try to inculcate in the Jewish people a certain attitude toward the human body, toward marriage, toward holiness, and toward God.

2

THE GOOD, THE BAD, AND THE HOLY

> A person should always go up in holiness and not go down.
>
> *Shabbat 21b*

TRADITIONAL JUDAISM paints a rather black and white picture of Jewish observance. An activity is either permitted (*mutar*) or forbidden (*asur*); a person is either obligated (*hiyav*) or not obligated (*patur*). The parameters of Jewish observance are clear.

Today, particularly in the area of sexual ethics, perhaps it makes more sense to speak in shades of gray. Rather than listing permitted and forbidden sexual activity, we ought to construct a new sexual ethic built on a ladder of holiness. Various kinds of sexual activity must be judged by where they stand on this ladder and how close they are to the Jewish ideal of holiness.

A ladder-type framework for sexual ethics has been suggested by Rabbi Arthur Green:

> Living in a world where we cannot advocate either ideal sex or no sex as the alternatives, what we must begin to evolve is a sliding scale of sexual values. (Rabbi Zalman Schachter is owed our thanks for first having articulated the notion of the "sliding scale" in various areas of neohalakhic practice.) At the top of this scale would stand the fully knowing and loving relationship . . . while rape—fully unconsenting and anonymous sexuality—would stand at the bottom. Somewhere

17

near the middle of the scale, neither glorified nor condemned, would
be the relationship of two consenting persons, treating one another
with decency, fulfilling the biological aspects of one another's love-
needs, while making no pretense at deeper intimacy. Given such a
scale, a Jew might begin to judge his/her own sexual behavior in terms
of a series of challenges which s/he might want to address.[1]

Even though one may disagree with the particular details of
Green's scale, a sliding scale of holiness seems the only model of
sexual ethics suitable for contemporary society. At the bottom of
the ladder are unethical and unacceptable types of sexual behavior;
at the top, sex that conforms to the Jewish ideal of holiness. In
between are various shades of gray.

MOVING UP THE LADDER

At the bottom of the ladder are unethical sexual relations. Let
us begin with this premise: if something is unethical or immoral,
it is immoral for all human beings, not simply for Jews. The rabbis
taught that all humankind (referred to as "the children of Noah")
are bound by certain basic ethical laws called the *sheva mitzvot
be-nai Noah*, "the seven commandments of the children of Noah":
"Seven commandments were commanded to the children of Noah,
establishing justice, the prohibition of blasphemy, idolatry, forbidden sexual relations, bloodshed, stealing, and eating the limb from
a living animal."[2] According to tradition, any gentile who follows
these basic laws has a place in the World to Come.

When describing these seven universal laws, the rabbis use the
term *gilui arayot* (literally, "uncovering nakedness") for forbidden
sexual relations, a broad term that could apply to a variety of
sexual activities. Throughout the Talmud the term *gilui arayot*
generally refers to two types of forbidden intercourse: incest and
adultery.[3] (In chapter 3 I will broaden the definition to include all
kinds of nonconsensual, exploitative, and destructive sexual relations.)

The next rung up the ladder is sexual activity between consenting, unmarried adults. Many of us would be hard pressed to call such sexual relations unethical. In fact, they can be quite loving and caring. The issue in nonmarital consensual sex is not *good* or *bad*, but *holy* or *not holy;* we have left the realm of ethics and entered the realm of holiness.[4] A variety of shades of gray fall within this distinction. At one extreme is promiscuity, sex with no pretense of a relationship, even anonymous sex. At the other is sex between two people in love, perhaps about to be married. As we shall see in chapter 4, Judaism, while not permissive, does not clearly condemn such sexual relations as it does incest and adultery.

Nonmarital consensual sex nevertheless falls short of the Jewish ideal of holiness. The Torah expects more of the Jewish people than simply ethical behavior; Judaism is not merely ethical monotheism. Judaism's demands go beyond being good to being holy, a theme reiterated numerous times in the Torah:

> The Lord spoke to Moses, saying: Speak to the whole Israelite community and say to them: You shall be holy, for I, the LORD your God, am holy. (Lev. 19:1–2)

> Now then, if you will obey me faithfully and keep My covenant . . . you shall be to Me a kingdom of priests and a holy nation. (Exod. 19:5–6)

> You shall be holy to Me, for I the LORD am holy, and I have set you apart from other peoples to be Mine. (Lev. 20:26)

In Judaism, sex becomes holy only within the context of marriage (see chapters 5 and 6). Let us look more deeply at the ideal of holiness in Judaism.

THE IDEA OF THE HOLY

Most modern Jews understand the concepts of good and evil, right and wrong, as they apply to daily activities. They have no difficulty with mitzvot such as "love your neighbor," "give to the poor," and "honor your parents." Holiness is a much more difficult concept to fathom. Perhaps that is why we frequently ignore those laws in Judaism meant to inculcate holiness; we don't fully understand the term.

I recall giving the opening invocation at a local public high school graduation ceremony. A Catholic priest was giving the closing benediction. The graduates were extremely rowdy and undisciplined, and the priest was unable to go ahead with his closing prayer. He turned to me and said, "The trouble with our young people is that they do not know the difference between the holy and the profane." He was right; in our secular, materialistic age, we seem to have lost our sense of the holy.

The Hebrew word for holy is *kadosh*; for holiness, *kedushah*. These terms literally mean "set apart" or special; some prefer the word "elevated."[5] *Kedushah* points to a level of reality beyond the physical. The following four examples from Jewish tradition illustrate this notion, each built upon the Hebrew root קָדוֹשׁ *kadosh*.

Physically, each day pretty much resembles another. The sun sets; the sun rises. There is a monotony to time. Yet Judaism teaches that one day in every seven has a special sanctity. We call these days Shabbat and mark them by beginning our dinner with a blessing over a glass of wine called קִידוּשׁ *kiddush*, or sanctification. On numerous other special days, each called *yom tov*, a holy day, we also chant the *kiddush*.

Physically, one piece of ground looks pretty much like any other. Yet one piece of ground on a hill in Jerusalem was chosen as the site of the מִקְדָשׁ *mikdash*, the holy Temple. Only one piece of that Temple is still standing, the Western wall, and Jews still honor the holiness of that group of stones.

Physically, one sexual relationship looks pretty much like another. Biologically the process is the same, whether the relationship is a casual pickup at a bar, an adulterous liaison at a hotel, a couple in love but not ready for the commitment of marriage, or a married couple sharing a bed as they build a home together. Yet in Judaism only the last relationship is called קִידוּשִׁין *kiddushin*, marriage—literally, holiness.

We are most victims of our physical selves when we confront death. The death of a loved one powerfully drives home the fact that we are flesh and blood. At that vulnerable time it is important to connect to the reality that extends beyond the physical by saying קַדִּישׁ *kaddish*; literally, we sanctify God's name. If God is holy, then we who are created in God's image are holy. There is more to us than our physical bodies.

Holiness, the realm beyond the physical, is central to Judaism. Jews have holy time, holy space, holy relationships, and a holy God. Our task as Jews is to connect ourselves to the realm of the holy by making *kedushah* part of our lives.

According to Judaism, being wise means being able to distinguish between the holy and the profane—*kodesh* and *ḥol*. This distinction is the essence of the *havdalah* prayer recited at the end of the Sabbath. The goal of the Jew is to bring holiness into one's day-to-day activities. In the words of Rabbi Joseph Soloveitchik, "Holiness is the descent of divinity into the midst of our concrete world."[6]

How is holiness achieved? The classical Jewish answer is through commandments. Before performing many of the commandments, a Jew recites a blessing: "Baruch Ata Adonai Elohenu Melech haolam Asher kidshanu be-mitzvotav ve-tzivanu _____." ("Praised are You, Lord our God, King of the universe, Who has made us holy with His commandments and commanded us _____.") Numerous commandments, particularly those pertaining to our relationship with God, have as their purpose helping us to achieve holiness. These include the observance of the Sabbath and festivals, the laws of synagogue worship, the recital of the Shema, the use of symbols such as the *tallit*, *tefillin*, and *mezuzah*, the recital of various daily blessings, and the observance of the dietary laws.

The dietary laws provide a clear example of how to achieve the ideal of holiness by sanctifying a basic physical activity. If the goal were merely to avoid unethical eating habits, then we would have to avoid only cruelty toward the animals one eats. (Not eating the limb of a living animal was one of the basic ethical laws given to the children of Noah.) We could eat almost anything and still be absolutely ethical. However, Judaism demands more: Jews are expected to limit their meat eating to certain animals, to ensure that those animals are slaughtered by carefully defined humane methods, to avoid eating the life-giving product of an animal (milk) with the flesh of an animal (meat), to say a proper blessing before and after eating, and to use the meal to discuss some words of Torah.[7] Obeying these laws helps Jews develop a certain reverence toward life and, ideally, a certain relationship with God.

From this example we begin to see how Jews are expected to achieve the ideal of holiness. First, they are guided by a discipline. The act of eating is sanctified through the discipline of the dietary laws. In a parallel way, the act of sex is sanctified through discipline. In Judaism, not having sex whenever one desires with whomever one desires, but limiting it instead to certain times and certain contexts, makes sexual intercourse a holy act.

Second, Judaism leads us to achieve holiness by striking a balance between two extremes, asceticism and hedonism. Western culture has tended to gravitate toward either of two extremes, the rejection of pleasure and the celebration of pleasure for its own sake. Judaism strives for a middle path. A Jewish text written for teens about the relationship between hedonism, asceticism, and holiness explains:

> A careful examination of mankind's past will demonstrate that basically there have been three approaches to answer the question: What shall I do with my life?

The first approach sees man as an animal and the world as a lush jungle to feast upon. This may be called the way of exploitation. [hedonism]

The second approach sees man as an angel and the world as an evil den to flee from. This may be called the way of escape. [asceticism]

The third approach differs from the other two. Instead of teaching exploitation or escape, it teaches encounter and sanctification. Instead of teaching that the world exists for the self, it teaches that the self exists for the world. It recognizes the situation as it really is, meets it and seeks to improve it. This may be called the way of sanctification or Judaism. [holiness]"[8]

Asceticism teaches that sex, or any physical pleasure, is tainted with evil and that the ideal is to avoid sex altogether. This approach has been extremely influential in Christianity. For example, Paul says to the Corinthians:

It is well for a man not to touch a woman. But because of the temptation to immorality, each man should have his own wife and each woman her own husband. The husband should give his wife her conjugal rights, and likewise the wife to her husband. . . .

Do not refuse one another, except perhaps by agreement for a season, that you may devote yourselves to prayer; but then come together again, lest Satan tempt you through lack of self-control. I say this by way of concession, not of command. I wish that all were as I myself am. But each has his own special gift from God, one of one kind and one of another.

To the unmarried and the widows I say that it is well for them to remain single as I do. But if they cannot exercise self-control, they should marry. For it is better to marry than to be aflame with passion.

To the married I give charge, not I but the Lord, that the wife should not separate from her husband (but if she does, let her remain single or else be reconciled to her husband) and that the husband should not divorce his wife. . . .

I think that in view of the impending distress it is well for a person to remain as he is. Are you bound to a wife? Do not seek to be free. Are you free from a wife? Do not seek marriage. But if you marry, you do not sin, and if a girl marries she does not sin. Yet those who marry will have worldly troubles, and I would spare you that. . . .

A wife is bound to her husband as long as he lives. If the husband dies, she is free to be married to whom she wishes only in the Lord. But in my judgment she is happier if she remains as she is. And I think that I have the Spirit of God. (1 Cor. 7)

In fairness to Paul, he was expecting the imminent Second Coming and the End of Days when he preached these words. He was also reacting to far more ascetic sects that eschewed any sexuality. Nevertheless, his approach became extremely influential in Christian theology. Because of these views, many people in our Western culture associate sex with sin and depravity. Today many Christian theologians are struggling with the implications of this ascetic tradition for modern Christianity.[9]

Judaism rejects the ascetic view toward sex. Holiness is not achieved through celibacy. Jewish tradition contains the powerful statement, "In the World to Come a man must give an accounting for every legitimate pleasure which he denied himself."[10] Sex is viewed as a vital part of God's creation; it is good and meant to be enjoyed.

In contrast to the ascetic view, modern secular culture has emphasized a hedonistic approach to sex. This is best exemplified by the *Playboy* philosophy that man's purpose in life is to maximize pleasure. To quote Hugh Hefner, publisher of *Playboy*:

Sex is a function of the body, a drive which man shares with animals, like eating, drinking and sleeping; it is a physical demand that must be satisfied. If you do not satisfy it, you will have all kinds of neuroses and repression psychoses. Sex is here to stay. Let us forget the prudery that makes us hide from it, throw away those inhibitions, find a girl who is like-minded and let yourself go.[11]

The hedonistic approach focuses on the animal-like aspects of human beings. Judaism rejects this view, teaching that humans are qualitatively different from animals. Although pleasure is important in Judaism, it must serve a higher purpose. An important talmudic passage notes the distinction between pleasure for its own sake and pleasure for a higher purpose:

> How does one explain these verses that contradict one another? It is written, "I therefore praised enjoyment (simha). [For the only good a man can have under the sun is to eat and drink and enjoy himself.]" (Ecc. 8:15) and it is written, "[Of revelry I said, It's mad!] Of merriment (simha): What good is that?" (Ecc. 2:2). There is no contradiction. [The first verse] is pleasure that comes with the commandments, [the second verse] is pleasure that does not come with commandments. This teaches us that God's presence does not dwell in sadness or laziness or play or levity, or conversation or small talk, but rather in the joy of the commandments.[12]

True pleasure in Judaism is tied to mitzvot, the fulfillment of God's will.

Holiness is achieved by walking a middle road between asceticism and hedonism. It comes through discipline, through the understanding that pleasure comes through observing the commandments, and through making an act special and set apart. Judaism claims that sex attains this level of holiness only within the context of marriage. Even within marriage there are rules regarding proper sexual behavior between a husband and wife.

Outside of marriage there is also a ladder of holiness in sexual relations. The goal of each Jew is to climb that ladder. And along the way are certain experiences that detract from holiness and others that enhance it.

DETRACTING FROM HOLINESS: PROSTITUTION, PROMISCUITY, AND PORNOGRAPHY

Both animals and humans perform sexual acts. For an animal such acts are purely biological, driven by instinct. Only humans can raise the sexual act above the biological level, giving it a spiritual quality. As we have already learned, striving toward holiness means elevating what would otherwise be only a biological act. It is what separates animals from human beings.

Sex as a purely physical act outside the context of a relationship detracts from holiness. The rabbis have a word for such sexual activity: *zenut*, often translated as promiscuity; it comes from the word *zonah*, which means prostitute.

From biblical times through the talmudic period and right up to the present, prostitution has been a fact of life. Not without reason is it called the world's oldest profession; every society has had its prostitutes, and Jews have been no exception. The Bible speaks of Tamar's harlotry (Gen. 38:12–19) and Rahab's professional prostitution (Josh. 2) without passing moral judgment.

Nevertheless, the Bible regarded the prostitute as far removed from the holiness ideal of Judaism. In the beautiful holiness chapter of Leviticus, Israel is warned, "Do not degrade your daughter and make her a harlot, lest the land fall into harlotry and the land be filled with depravity" (Lev. 19:29). A priest was forbidden from marrying a *zonah* (Lev. 21:7). Perhaps most important, sacred prostitution was forbidden in the ancient Temple. The Torah teaches, "No Israelite woman shall be a cult prostitute, nor shall any Israelite man be a cult prostitute" (Deut. 23:18). This prohibition contrasts sharply with practices of the other nations among whom the Israelites lived, in which cultic prostitutes were the norm.

The prophets of Israel denounced prostitutes. The Book of Proverbs, traditionally attributed to Solomon, warns against consorting with prostitutes:

> From the window of my house,
> Through the lattice, I looked out.
> And saw among the simple, noticed among the youths,
> A lad devoid of sense.
> He was crossing the street near her corner,
> Walking toward her house.

In the dusk of evening, in the dark hours of night.
A woman comes toward him
Dressed like a harlot with set purpose.
She is bustling and restive; she is never at home.
Now in the street, now in the square,
She lurks at every corner.
She lays hold of him and kisses him.
Brazenly she says to him,
I had to make a sacrifice of well-being;
Today I fulfilled my vows.
Therefore I have come out to you,
Seeking you, and have found you.
I have decked my couch with covers of dyed Egyptian linen;
I have sprinkled my bed with myrrh, aloes, and cinnamon.
Let us drink our fill of love till morning;
Let us delight in amorous embrace.
For the man of the house is away,
He is off on a distant journey.
He took his bag of money with him
And will return only at mid-month.
She sways him with her eloquence,
Turns him aside with her smooth talk.
Thoughtlessly he follows her,
Like an ox going to the slaughter,
Like a fool to the stocks for punishment—
Until the arrow pierces his liver.
He is like a bird rushing into a trap,
Not knowing his life is a stake.

(Prov. 7:6–23)

For the prophets, the prostitute became the symbol of Israel gone astray from worshiping one God. Prostitution may have been acknowledged as a fact of life, but it was considered the antithesis of holiness.

The rabbis of the Talmud also warned about visiting prostitutes. In recognition of the reality of prostitution in their society, they did permit the wages of a prostitute to be used for the Temple.[13] However, a man was expected to strive for a higher ideal; he was forbidden to approach a harlot's door or pass through a harlot's market.[14]

In biblical times, the word *zonah* meant either a cultic prostitute or a professional harlot. The rabbis, however, broadened the meaning of the term. For example, the prohibition of a priest marrying a *zonah* led to the following discussion:

> "Zonah" implies, as her name [indicates, a faithless wife]: so said Rabbi Eliezer. Rabbi Akiba said: Zonah means one who is a prostitute. Rabbi Mattiah ben Heresh said: Even a woman whose husband, while going to arrange for her drinking [i.e., the ordeal of the sotah], cohabited with her on the way is rendered a zonah. Rabbi Judah said: Zonah implies one who is incapable of procreation. And the sages said: Zonah is none other than a female proselyte, a freed bondwoman, and one who has been subject to any biblically forbidden intercourse.
>
> Rabbi Elazar said: An unmarried man who had intercourse with an unmarried woman with no matrimonial intent, renders her thereby a zonah. Rabbi Amram said: The halakhah is not in agreement with the opinion of Rabbi Elazar.[15]

Here the Talmud gives six definitions of *zonah*. The law accepts the opinion of the sages: a *zonah* is a female proselyte, a freed bondwoman, and one who has been subject to any biblically forbidden intercourse.

The rabbis were generally willing to presume that a man does not have sexual relations for purposes of *zenut*, translated as promiscuity.[16] On the other hand, occasionally when it met their purposes, they overlooked this presumption. For example, when a man betrothed a woman improperly, the rabbis were willing to annul the betrothal retroactively and declare the sexual relation *zenut*.

In the passage quoted above, the rabbis broadened the definition of *zenut* from actual prostitution to any form of promiscuity.

Rabbi Elazar tried to broaden it still further to include all sexual relations between unmarried adults, but his opinion is rejected. The strong reaction to Rabbi Elazar's statement seems to indicate that the rabbis excluded certain sexual encounters between non-married adults from the category of *zenut*.

The Rambam (Maimonides), in his great code of Jewish law, follows Rabbi Elazar. According to him, *zenut* refers to any non-marital sex. The Ravad (Rabbi Avraham ben David) sharply disagrees: "A *kadesha* [another term for prostitute] means only when she is promiscuous and sleeps with any man."[17]

A modern definition of *zenut* would follow the sages and the Ravad to include any sexual activity performed on a purely biological or animal level. According to this rabbinic model, *zenut* is the opposite of holiness. It is sex as purely physical release, with no pretense of a relationship. Long ago the rabbis recognized that *zenut* is destructive to society.

Zenut includes prostitution. Almost every modern society has outlawed prostitution as destructive to the moral fiber of a society. Certainly modern-day prostitution, with its connections to drugs, disease, teenage runaways, pimps, and the underworld, is anathema to Jewish morality.

Zenut also includes promiscuity. Although promiscuity cannot be outlawed, it can be condemned. The spread of venereal disease, the rise in teenage pregnancies, and the cavalier attitude toward sex in the popular media are all the unfortunate fruits of promiscuity. It is up to our churches and synagogues as well as our schools to teach that promiscuity is destructive to society.

Pornography, in which sex is photographed or filmed for sale, also comes under the rubric of *zenut*. In many ways, pornography resembles prostitution; both involve the exchange of money for sex. The issue of pornography is complicated by the secondary issue of censorship and First Amendment rights; nevertheless, pornography has been attacked not only on religious grounds but by feminists who claim that it demeans women and by social analysts who claim that it contributes to violence of society.

One contemporary commentator who has written extensively and cogently on this issue, Dennis Prager, claims that social and feminist arguments against pornography are specious.[18] Women who pose for pornography, he argues, do so willingly and freely, are often highly compensated, and see their posing as a stepping-stone in their career. What this minority of women do cannot be considered demeaning to the majority of women who choose not to participate. As for the issue of violence, Prager writes that some of the most violent societies on earth have been some of the most prudish, in which pornography and even public immodesty were totally forbidden.

Prager condemns pornography not for its effects on women but for what it does to men: it becomes addictive. He writes:

> Is it really possible that viewing hundreds or thousands of perfect looking naked women has no effect on the way a man sees his wife or girl friend, or women generally? After "making love" to the perfect looking women of pornography, will a man be just as likely to find his imperfect looking woman as sexually desirable, as feminine?[19]

Pornography is destructive because it gives men unrealistic expectations. It undermines a man's ability to form a stable relationship with a woman, such relationships being the building blocks of our society.

Prager ends his essay with a familiar theme, that pornography undermines holiness:

> As is the case in all adult consensual sexual activity—extramarital, homosexual, orgiastic, and even incestuous—the only real argument against pornography, too, is that it is unholy. Only a religious world-view can truly argue that pornography demeans. In a secular society such as ours, wherein posing naked is often honored, the argument that pornographic models are demeaned is specious.

In the final analysis, there are very few secular arguments against pornography. In a society that denies the transcendent, the physical is the one reality. The only violence it understands, therefore, is violence committed against the body—and that is where the society will direct its concern. The violence of pornography, however, is not against the body. It is against the divine image within us, against the soul—of the model, of the user, and of society. But a society that does not believe in a soul cannot make that argument.[20]

Prager's words can be broadened to include all sex performed for purely physical release. Pornography recognizes only our animal bodies, not our holy spirit. It may be ethical in that it does not hurt anybody, but it does violence against the divine soul. That is why *zenut*, in all its modern manifestations—prostitution, promiscuity, and pornography—destroys the holiness ideal of Judaism.

ENHANCING HOLINESS: MODESTY

Holiness is what separates humans from the animal kingdom. Animals copulate without respect to where they are or who sees them. For humans, modesty and privacy enhance the holiness of sexual relations. This basic Jewish attitude can be traced back to the garden of Eden, where Adam and Eve lived an animal-like existence: "The two of them were naked, the man and his wife, yet they felt no shame" (Gen. 2:25). They had not yet eaten from the tree of knowledge; they were innocents, as animals are innocents.

By eating of the tree, humans separated themselves from the animal kingdom: "Then the eyes of both of them were opened and they perceived that they were naked; and they sewed together fig leaves and made themselves loincloths" (Gen. 3:7). According to Jewish tradition the sin of Adam and Eve was not sex; it was disobedience of God's word. Once they gained knowledge, Adam and Eve lost their innocence. Yet they gained something else: the ability to achieve holiness.

The Hebrew word for modesty is *tzniyut*.[21] The laws of *tzniyut* are most prominent in the traditional dress codes of Judaism, in which one is generally forbidden to expose parts of the body that are usually covered. Although modesty in dress is important for both women and men, women in particular have traditionally been taught the laws of *tzniyut*. The Talmud gives a number of rules:

> Rav Hisda said, A woman's leg is *ervah* (sexually suggestive). . . . Shmuel said, A woman's voice is *ervah*. . . . Rav Sheshet said, A woman's hair is *ervah*.[22]

Another statement on the same page takes the laws of *tzniyut* much further. "Anyone who looks even at the baby finger of a woman, it is as if he looked at her private parts." These early standards of public modesty strongly affected the dress codes of Jewish men and women throughout the generations. Even today many pious Jews keep them with great scrupulousness.

Other Jews argue that standards of modesty change from age to age and society to society. Uncovering a woman's hair or hearing a woman's voice may not be sexually suggestive in our modern culture. Nevertheless, even those who advocate a more liberal interpretation of these guidelines would agree that the public uncovering of genitals, or even the exposure of too much skin, violates the Jewish ideal of modesty and holiness. Though the details may change, the overall principle of *tzniyut* remains even in our own generation.

The rabbis taught that *tzniyut* in Judaism is not related simply to dress but is a far broader term that refers to modesty and discretion in all areas of sexual activity. The sex life between a husband and wife should never be open for public discussion, the only exceptions being with a therapist during counseling or with a physician when necessary. Obviously, in these cases professional confidentiality is the rule. In addition, it is inappropriate to brag about one's sexual conquests, to describe one's sexual life, or to have sex in any place where others can see it. This is why pornography is so foreign to Jewish values.

Another example of *tzniyut* is found in the observance of the laws of family purity and *mikvah* (see chapter 5). Among traditional Jews, a woman immerses in the *mikvah* once a month following a period of separation from her husband and then resumes sex with him. A woman never tells anybody except her husband when she goes to the *mikvah,* and the *mikvah* attendant is expected to exercise absolute privacy and discretion. Sex between a husband and wife, although beautiful and holy, is not public information.

Modesty is the classical Jewish way to enhance the holiness of the sexual act. In ancient times, it separated the Jews from the Hellenists, who held athletic contests in the nude and worshiped the beauty of the human body. Today it separates Jews from many of their secular contemporaries, whose sexual lives have become topics for locker room and cocktail party conversation, and celebrity memoirs. If holiness means "set apart" or "special," sex becomes holy when it is protected by a fence of modesty and discretion.

ENHANCING HOLINESS: LOVE

If holiness is what elevates human sex above animal sex, then it is achieved only in the context of a relationship. An animal in heat will have sex with the nearest available partner. Only humans can limit their sexual activity to one special person or, to use popular terminology, animals "have sex"; only human beings can "make love."

Judaism has always recognized the beauty and value of love between a man and a woman. The Bible writes:

Let me be a seal upon your heart, /Like the seal upon your hand.
For love is fierce as death, /Passion is mighty as Sheol;

Its darts are darts of fire, /A blazing flame.
Vast floods cannot quench love, /Nor rivers drown it.
If a man offered all his wealth for love,
He would be laughed to scorn.

(Song of Songs 8:6–7)

The rabbis added their own thoughts about love: "When love is strong, a man and woman can make their bed on a sword's blade. When love grows weak, a bed of sixty cubits is not large enough."[23] To Jews, the love between a man and a woman has never been regarded as a pure spiritual state separate from the physical act of sex. The Jewish ideal has never been "to love pure and chaste from afar." Love and sex have always been intimately wrapped up with one another.

Robert Gordis expresses the physical and spiritual nature of love clearly:

> In a right and perfect union, the love of a man and a woman is, and should be, inseparable from sexual experience. The emotion of love which is spiritual expresses itself in sexual acts which are physical, so as to create total human participation. The sex-love relationship is not complete unless it is accompanied by a feeling of permanence. It is not an act of deception or even honest hyperbole that impels lovers to swear that their love will endure forever. What is deep and all-inclusive will not be satisfied without the conviction that it will endure.
>
> The love of a man and a woman expresses itself not only in a physical desire for each other but also by a sense of concern for one another, a desire to make the partner happy at any cost, even a major sacrifice.[24]

Gordis points out that to the medieval romantic, ideal love was chaste love, separated from sex. At the opposite extreme, the new morality speaks of sex without love, pleasure without commitment. Both views separate sex from love, the body from the soul. Both flow out of the Platonic dichotomy between the physical and the spiritual which has been so influential in our Western culture.

This dualistic view is foreign to Judaism, in which the love of a man and a woman finds its greatest expression in the sexual act. Sex approaches the holiness ideal within the context of love; love and sex are intimately connected.

In spite of the connection, there is a danger within our notion of love: our modern culture romanticizes it. Popular music, novels, and movies are obsessed with the search for romantic love, and too often what is idealized is love without responsibility. As a rabbi, I speak with young people about finding a life partner who shares their religion and their values, but they can speak only about falling in love. The attitude that "love conquers all" causes too many people to become involved in irresponsible and even destructive relationships.

Jewish tradition has always recognized the difference between responsible and irresponsible love. The rabbis teach:

> All love that is dependent on something else, if that something else disappears, the love disappears. All love that is not dependent on something else will never disappear. What is a love that is dependent on something else? The love between Amnon and Tamar. What is a love that is not dependent on something else? The love between David and Jonathan.[25]

In the story of Amnon and Tamar (2 Sam. 13), Amnon, the son of King David, becomes infatuated with his beautiful half-sister Tamar. He rapes her and, upon achieving satisfaction, loathes her. These sad events lead to conflict and treachery in King David's household, culminating in the revolt by Absalom, Tamar's full brother. This incident exemplifies irresponsible love at its worst or, perhaps more properly, sexual attraction masquerading as love.

The rabbis contrast this incident to the love between David and Jonathan. This is not sexual love, although many Jewish gay activists find sexual implications within the relationship between David and Jonathan. Theirs was a friendship built on an eternal love, characterized by the willingness to sacrifice for the beloved. Jonathan gives up the kingship to save David's life. His parting words to his friend are, "Go in peace! For we two have sworn to each other in the name of the LORD: 'May the LORD be [witness] between you and me, and between your offspring and mine, forever!' " (1 Sam. 20:42). Their friendship represents the ideal of responsible love.

Love in Judaism means the willingness to sacrifice for one's beloved. It means love with no ulterior motive and a commitment to permanence. It is responsible love, love with the head as well as the heart. The romantic ideal of "falling head over heels in love" is decidedly secondary in Judaism. Real love comes only with time, with moments of intimacy, and with shared values.

When Isaac meets his future wife Rebekah, the Torah says, "Isaac then brought her into the tent of his mother Sarah, and he took Rebekah as his wife. Isaac loved her, and thus found comfort after his mother's death" (Gen. 24:67). It is noteworthy that the marriage comes first, then the love. Real love can flourish in Judaism only within the context of marriage.

Our ladder of holiness in regard to sexual activity must reflect the notion that the greater the love, the higher the degree of holiness. Certainly sex between two close and intimate friends is higher on the ladder than sex between anonymous strangers. Sex with one's exclusive lover is higher still. The highest degree of holiness is reserved for the most permanent relationship: marriage. Within the marital relationship, love and sex are intimately tied together. Sex is a way of expressing love; love is a way of sanctifying sex.

3

SEX THAT DESTROYS

> For all transgressions in the Torah, if a man is told
> "transgress and do not die," he should transgress
> and not die except for idolatry, incest-adultery, and
> murder.
>
> *Sanhedrin 74a*

THE WOMAN who came to see me was in her late thirties, deeply depressed, unable to form a stable relationship with a man. As a young girl and through her early teenage years, she had been a victim of incest and rape at the hands of a family member. She had written a bitter, anonymous letter to the local Jewish community newspaper chastising Jews for their attitude that "rape is not a Jewish problem." I had responded to the letter and offered her rabbinic counseling. Admittedly I was somewhat surprised when she called me.

I saw a deeply unhappy and troubled woman. "I feel unclean even coming to see you. You are a rabbi, you represent God. How can I step into a synagogue when this has happened to me? How can God forgive me? Rape is not supposed to happen in good Jewish families." She shared with me a sordid tale of incest and abuse, of family members who preferred to turn their backs while she was victimized. More than twenty years later, she was still traumatized, unable to discuss her past with members of her family and bitter at the Jewish community. "The community does nothing for people like me!"

She needed more intensive counseling than I could give her.

Fortunately, she has found a good therapist and has begun to make progress. I urged her to approach the local Jewish family service agency about starting a support group for victims of rape and incest. I hope I have convinced her that she is not unclean, that she is a victim, and that there is one rabbi who will always be there for her.

The truth is that sex can hurt and destroy. Judaism from its very beginnings has recognized that some sexual acts are unethical; that is why the rabbis identified the sexual drive with the evil inclination. Used improperly, it has the potential for great evil. When the rabbis laid down seven fundamental ethical laws incumbent on all human beings, one of the laws forbade unethical sex.[1] Later, when the rabbis laid down three fundamental laws of Judaism for which it is better to die than transgress, unethical sex was among them.

In my rabbinic counseling, I have seen the power of sex to destroy. I spoke with a woman who had been married for more than twenty-five years when her husband ran off with a younger woman, abandoning her with two teenage children and no source of income. She came to me after they were divorced and she was struggling to make ends meet. She told me, "Rabbi, tell people that adultery destroys. It destroyed my family."

A college student who was pregnant and trying to decide her future related, "He told me he loved me. He told me we would be forever. Then the minute I got pregnant he fled. It was no longer his responsibility." The young man wanted the physical pleasure of sex but fled from the responsibility. He used words of love to get sex, but his action toward his girlfriend was anything but loving.

Before I explore more deeply the Jewish issues regarding unethical sex, two conclusions from previous chapters are worth repeating. First, if something is unethical, it is unethical for all human beings, not just for Jews. We cannot say that a particular activity is morally wrong for Jews but morally correct if done by non-Jews. Jews are included in the seven basic ethical mitzvot given to all human beings.

Second, sexual activity between two unmarried, consenting adults is not necessarily unethical. On the contrary, such activity can be quite caring and ethical. If Jewish law forbids nonmarital sex, the reason has more to do with its ideal of holiness than with ethics. (Similarly, Jewish law forbids eating pork, but few would say that a Jew who eats pork is acting unethically.) We muddle the issue when we use terms like "immoral" and "unethical" for activities that do not hurt and destroy.

In chapter 4, I discuss the issue of nonmarital sex. This chapter is concerned with sex that destroys. Unfortunately, there is too much of it in our society.

WHAT IS UNETHICAL SEX?

Sol Gordon and Judith Gordon have written an excellent book for parents that deals with moral issues in sex education while avoiding an explicitly religious stand.[2] The authors list what they consider the seven deadly sins of immoral sex:

1. rape, molestation, and sexual assault;
2. hurting, forcing, deceiving, exploiting, and corrupting;
3. sexually irresponsible behavior (such as a man abandoning a pregnant woman);
4. perpetuating the double standard;
5. sex stereotyping;
6. sexual harassment of women; and
7. lying to young children about the facts of life.[3]

It is difficult to disagree with the Gordons' list. Certainly any of these activities are hurtful to other human beings and represent transgressions of the Golden Rule, "Love your neighbor as yourself" (Lev. 19:18). Both Judaism and Christianity endorse the notion that human beings are created in God's image, and anything that hurts or diminishes the dignity of a human being is an affront to God.

Traditional Jewish sources do not supply a specific list like the Gordons'. Tradition uses the broad term *gilui arayot*, literally, "uncovering nakedness," to refer to unethical sex. Although there is some debate about the precise understanding of the term, *gilui arayot* is generally understood to refer to adultery and incest.

What do adultery and incest have in common? Both attack the very foundation of the family. Adultery undermines the basic trust on which the marital bond is built. Incest undermines the trust relationship between child and parent or brother and sister. Both can destroy the family, which according to the Torah is the basic building block of society. Incest also creates the potential for exploitation because it involves two people in the same household, one of whom may be dependent upon the other.

From a traditional Jewish perspective, *unethical sex is sex that destroys families.* It undermines the delicate trust relationships on which families are built. Even if incest occurs between knowledgeable, consenting adults, and even if adultery occurs with one's partner's consent, Judaism would find such liaisons abominations. That is why Joseph tells Potiphar's wife that adultery is "a sin against God" (Gen. 39:9).

The Gordons' list differs in an interesting way from the treatment of unethical sex in classical Jewish sources. The Gordons, taking a secular point of view, leave out of their list both adultery and incest. (In fairness, they do devote a whole section of their book to the sexual abuse of children by members of their own family.) More surprising, Jewish sources do not deal with the kind of unethical activity listed by the Gordons. Even rape is not a major concern of the rabbis, as we shall see. These omissions perhaps reflect the attitude that Jews do not do these things; therefore, it is unnecessary to discuss them.

Some contemporary Jews have tried to broaden the definition of *gilui arayot* to include other kinds of unethical or exploitative behavior. A recent article in *Reconstructionist* magazine pointed out, for instance, that *ervah* (from the same root as *arayot*) has no English equivalent:

> Our ervah is a place in our bodies, the place where Adam and Eve put their fig leaves. But ervah is also a place on our souls. The ervah is our soft spot, the hidden, absolutely vulnerable place where our body and soul meet.[4]

Gilui arayot is sex in which the soft spot is uncovered and left exposed:

> Very simply, it means making a person completely vulnerable, and then not taking care of them in their nakedness.
>
> There is, I think, a powerful lesson for us in these words: know that when you have sex, you are uncovering the most private, most fragile part of your body and your soul. Do you trust this person with your soul's soft spot? Do you trust yourself with theirs? If not, our sacred language tells us, leave it covered.[5]

Sex exposes the most vulnerable parts of both our bodies and our souls. It puts us into a position in which we can easily be deeply hurt. I have met individuals whose sexual development has been stifled by an unkind remark about sexual performance by an early partner. Sex with the wrong partner, when one is too young, when one is vulnerable, or when there is lack of trust, can scar a person for life.

Sex, because it involves an intimate relationship when we are most vulnerable, demands an ethic of loving and caring. It requires delicacy, a sensitivity to one's partner's needs, discretion, and privacy. It involves choosing a partner who is emotionally mature. Teenagers as a rule are not ready for sex.

We return, then, to our original question: what is unethical sex? It certainly includes certain broad categories of sexual misbehavior: rape, incest, and adultery. In general, unethical sex can be defined as any sexual act that hurts another by taking advantage of his or her vulnerability. We can hurt another human being profoundly with our sexual organs. This violation is what is meant by the prohibition of *gilui arayot* —"exposing one's nakedness"—one of the seven basic ethical laws given to all human beings.

RAPE AND INCEST

Today we understand rape not as a sexual act but as an act of violence. The rapist wants more than sexual satisfaction; he wants to dominate the woman he rapes. Often rape is motivated as much by hatred of women as by love of sex.

Traditional Jewish law has no such understanding of rape. The Torah mentions rape only within the context of adultery:

> If a man is found lying with another man's wife, both of them—the man and the woman with whom he lay—shall die. Thus you will sweep away evil from Israel.
>
> In the case of a virgin who is engaged to a man—if a man comes upon her in town and lies with her, you shall take the two of them out to the gate of that town and stone them to death: the girl because she did not cry for help in the town, and the man because he violated his neighbor's wife. Thus you will sweep away evil from your midst. But if a man comes upon the engaged girl in the open country, and the man lies with her by force, only the man who lay with her shall die, but you shall do nothing to the girl. The girl did not incur the death penalty, for this case is like that of a man attacking another and murdering him. He came upon her in the open; though the engaged girl cried for help, there was no one to save her.
>
> If a man comes upon a virgin who is not engaged and he seizes her and lies with her, and they are discovered, the man who lay with her shall pay the girl's father fifty [shekels of] silver, and she shall be his wife. Because he has violated her, he can never have the right to divorce her. (Deut. 22:22–29)

The Torah has only two concerns. The first involves the rape of a betrothed woman, when the bridesprice has been paid and the couple are legally bound to one another. In this case, is the rape adultery? If it occurs in the field, then the presumption is that the woman cried out and nobody heard her; therefore, she is not guilty. If the rape occurs in the city, then the presumption is that she did not cry out but participated willingly; therefore, she is guilty.

The second issue concerns the rape of an unbetrothed virgin. In that case the man is forced to marry her and loses his absolute right to divorce. The concern is with the financial loss to her family by the loss of the woman's virginal status, as well as with her difficulty in finding another husband. In a later period, the rabbis ruled that the rapist is forced to marry her only if she and her father agree.[6] If he does not marry her, he must pay not only a fine but damages for her injury, blemish, and pain.[7]

According to Rachel Biale, rape as we know it is unknown in the Bible:

> Rape was not seen as a crime of sexual assault against a random woman because she is female, but rather as a calculated attempt by a man to acquire a woman as his wife against her and her parents' wishes. Thus rape is analogous to illegal seizure.[8]

For this reason, the Bible never discusses the rape of a married woman; the rape of a betrothed woman is discussed only within the context of adultery.

In the Talmud, the only issue in the case of rape is the possibility of adultery. According to traditional Jewish law, a woman who commits adultery is forbidden both to her husband and her paramour. What about a woman who is raped? The Talmud teaches:

> The father of Samuel taught: a woman who is raped is forbidden to her husband, perhaps the beginning was by force but in the end she went along willingly. . . . This disagrees with Rava, for Rava ruled: In all cases where the beginning is by force and in the end she goes along willingly, even if she says [to her rescuers] leave him alone, if this had

not happened I would have hired him, she is permitted to her husband. What is the reason? Her sexual drive overpowered her.[9]

Jewish law follows Rava and not the father of Samuel. A woman who is raped is permitted to her husband, even if in the end she went along willingly. The only exception is the wife of a Kohen. A Kohen, in order to maintain ritual purity, has special restrictions placed upon his sexual partners. By traditional Jewish law, if his wife is raped, or even if she is abducted and there is suspicion of rape, he must divorce her.

These sources seem archaic to modern Jews. As mentioned, rape as a crime of violence was unknown to Jewish sources. It was a concern to the rabbis only in that it might affect the status of a married or betrothed woman. Does Judaism nonetheless give us insights about rape that we can apply to our modern society?

Indeed it does. First, the rabbis took the crime of rape quite seriously. In a discussion about the permissibility of taking someone's life to prevent him from committing a crime, the Mishnah teaches, "These can be saved (from committing a transgression) even at the cost of their life: one who pursues his fellow to kill him, who pursues a man (for homosexual rape), or who pursues a betrothed maiden (to rape her)."[10] (The case of the betrothed maiden is the only example of rape in the Torah.)

Judaism places an infinite value on human life. The law that permits the slaying of a pursuer (rodef) to prevent murder is understandable, but the fact that the Mishnah also countenances the slaying of a rodef to prevent a rape shows how heinous the tradition considered the crime. (Interestingly, Judaism never allows the taking of a life to prevent a crime against property.) Rape is compared to murder, a crime against a person's very being.

A second insight comes from Rava's opinion, quoted above. A woman is never blamed for the rape, even if in the end she went along willingly. Even in modern society, we tend to blame the victim in rape cases. Recently, a rapist in Florida was found innocent when a jury ruled that the victim's provocative dress was a contributing factor. Often a rape victim is questioned about her past sexual experiences. From Rava's ruling we can extrapolate the Jewish view that a woman's dress, past sexual experiences, or even her relationship to the man who raped her are irrelevant. When the sexual act takes place without consent, it is rape.

This attitude pertains even to marital rape. Some modern legal sources debate whether a man can rape his own wife or whether the marital status gives him an absolute right to sex with her even without her consent. Judaism is clear on this issue: "Rami b. Hama, citing R. Assi, further ruled: A man is forbidden to compel his wife to the marital obligation."[11]

If rape is forbidden between husband and wife, it is even more so between two acquaintances. Most rapes are not committed by a stranger but by an individual who knows the victim. Often they occur on a date or between two people romantically involved, so-called date rape. Sometimes a man compels a woman too young to consent to sexual relations—statutory rape. Any time sex involves compulsion or anything less than full consent, it is rape and is therefore condemned by Jewish sources.

Some of the worst cases of rape occur within a family, when children are subjected to sexual abuse by their own parents, siblings, or other relatives. Victims are often scarred for decades to come. Contrary to popular belief, such abuse does happen in Jewish families. Let us look more closely at the incest taboo and Jewish law.

The most serious sexual prohibition in the Torah is incest. Two chapters in the book of Leviticus are devoted to forbidden sexual relations within the family. When a person is born, a whole series of individuals become forbidden sexually. When he or she marries, numerous members of the spouse's family become forbidden. Most of the prohibitions remain in effect even if the individual is widowed or divorced. For example, a man is forbidden to his father's wife (his stepmother) even after his father dies.

Below is a list of forbidden sexual relations for a man (a parallel list can be made for a woman):

1. his mother (Lev. 18:7);
2. his stepmother (Lev. 18:7);
3. his sister, including his half-sister (Lev. 18:9);
4. his daughter (Lev. 18:10 actually mentions only his granddaughter; the rabbis infer his daughter from this.);
5. his biological aunt (Lev. 18:12,13);
6. his uncle's wife (Lev. 18:14);
7. his son's wife (Lev. 18:15);
8. his brother's wife (Lev. 18:16. An exception is made when a man dies childless and the brother takes on the obligation of Levirate marriage. This has fallen out of practice in Judaism.);
9. his stepdaughter or mother-in-law (Lev. 18:17);
10. two sisters (Lev. 18:18. After the death of the first sister, the second may be married.).

The rabbis expanded the list to include a number of secondary prohibitions known as *shniyot*, which include such relatives as a man's grandmother, his great-granddaughter, and his grandson's wife. What is fascinating are the relations that are not forbidden, which include marriage between stepbrother and -sister, an uncle and a niece, or first cousins. Some of these marriages, although permissible by Jewish law, have been forbidden by the societies where Jews live, including Israel.

The only reason given by the Torah for these prohibitions is to separate the Israelites from the nations among whom they lived: "You shall not copy the practices of the land of Egypt where you dwelt, or of the land of Canaan to which I am taking you, nor shall you follow their laws. . . . None of you shall come near anyone of his own flesh to uncover nakedness: I am the LORD" (Lev. 18:3,6). Incest was a common practice within the culture of ancient Canaan, as were cult prostitution and fertility rituals.

The incest taboo is almost universal in societies today, partly because of the fear of genetic abnormalities among children of blood relatives. Such fears, however, do not explain the prohibition of a man's marrying his son's ex-wife. Maimonides gives his own explanation:

> The female relatives whom a man may not marry are alike in this respect—that as a rule they are constantly together with him in his house; they would easily listen to him, and do what he desires; they are near at hand, and he would have no difficulty in procuring them. No judge could blame him if found in their company. If to these relatives the same law applied as to all other unmarried women, if we were allowed to marry any of them, and were only precluded from sexual intercourse with them without marriage, most people would constantly have become guilty of misconduct with them.[12]

To Maimonides, the potential for exploitation when two people live in the same household is sufficient reason for the strong prohibition.

Today, most cases of incest involve minor children raped or molested by a parent, stepparent, older sibling, or other relative. Contrary to the popular myth, such incest is not uncommon in the Jewish community. It does occur in Jewish families; children who are victims can be affected for life. Incest victims often have low self-esteem and cannot trust members of the opposite sex or establish satisfactory sexual relationships as adults. If a father molests his young daughter, she often feels great anger against her mother for allowing the incest to happen.

The Jewish community must reach out to Jewish victims of sexual abuse. Jewish family service agencies can set up outreach programs and support groups for such individuals. Therapy groups, besides helping victims build self-esteem, dissipate anger, and reestablish trust, can also help victims of sexual abuse realize that the community cares. Unfortunately, embarrassment, lack of funds, and an attitude that "it doesn't happen in Jewish families" have prevented such groups from forming in many cities.

ADULTERY

An old joke often told by rabbis is that Moses comes down from the mountain carrying the two tablets and says, "I have good news and bad news. The good news is—I got Him down to ten. The bad news is—adultery is still out."

Adultery is as old as the human race. A midrash says that Cain slew Abel because they were fighting over who would sleep with Eve, their mother and Adam's wife. One of Judaism's earliest goals was to protect the integrity of marriage. Basic to the religious outlook are the sanctity of marriage and the importance of fidelity. If the ideal is that "a man leaves his father and mother and clings to his wife, so that they become one flesh" (Gen. 2:24), then to cling to another on the side goes against God's plan for humankind.

When I teach teens in my synagogue, I often do an exercise called "You're the rabbi. How would you handle this situation?" One question I ask is about a couple who want to be married but to have an open marriage, each with the right to keep other lovers on the side. The youngsters always answer that if they were the rabbi, they would not perform such a marriage. Even these teens understand that a Jewish marriage demands fidelity.

Adultery is the only sexual transgression mentioned in the Ten Commandments. The Torah makes it a capital crime for both the woman who commits adultery and her lover, and it is one of three transgressions for which it is better to die than to transgress. The Ten Commandments even outlaw coveting another's wife.

Nonetheless adultery is prevalent in our society. Rabbi Maurice Lamm writes that, in our pleasure-oriented society, marital fidelity may be a virtue of the past for most people:

> Superficially, fidelity does seem old-fashioned. It denies that the only excitement in love is that of a stranger, and that happiness is the only worthwhile goal. It denies that "I" am the most important person in the world, and that "experiencing" is the chief value in life. It denies that the great lover is the multiple lover, and that the satisfactions of a moment are more valuable than the lasting relationship of a lifetime. But if fidelity is dismissed as an irrelevant ideal, then marriage, which demands fidelity in order to survive, must also be thrown away.[13]

In Judaism, adultery is the ultimate crime against a family. As a rabbi, I have seen too many marriages crash on the shoals of an affair. It is vital that rabbis today make a statement that adultery is wrong.

I find three problems in the classical Jewish view toward adultery:

1. There is a double standard. Traditional Jewish law defines adultery as a sexual encounter between a married woman and a man not her husband. An affair between a married man and a single woman is not considered adultery.
2. Jewish law leaves no room for forgiveness. The rabbis have ruled that when a woman commits adultery, she is forbidden both to her lover and her husband.[14]
3. By Jewish law, the child of an adulterous relationship bears the parents' stigma, as does a child of incest. He or she becomes a *mamzer* and is forbidden to marry a Jew of legitimate birth.

Let us deal with all three issues. As for the double standard, in the original sources Jewish marriage was not egalitarian. In biblical times, a man was permitted to have more than one wife or to have a wife and a concubine. Obviously, there could be no prohibition on a man having sexual partners other than his wife as long as the partners were not married to someone else.

On the other hand, a married woman was "set aside" for her husband—the literal meaning of the word for marriage, *kiddushin*. (*Kadosh* means "holy" but also "set apart.")[15] Furthermore, a man could not only have more than one wife but could divorce his wife against her will.

In spite of the early double standard, a look at Jewish marriage from a historical perspective reveals an evolution toward greater equality between husband and wife. The Talmud strongly discourages polygamy. In the Middle Ages the rabbis outlawed it altogether. Similarly, in talmudic times the rabbis limited the ability of a man to divorce his wife unilaterally, requiring him to pay a large sum of money called a *ketubbah*. By the Middle Ages, the rabbis had ruled that a woman could not be divorced against her will at all. Although even today Jewish marital law is not totally egalitarian, there has been a definite trend in that direction.

In talmudic sources we see the trend toward marital egalitarianism in the treatment of extramarital sex. The best example is the law of the *sotah*. In the Torah, if a man suspected his wife of committing adultery, he could put her through a trial by ordeal in which she was forced to drink bitter waters. If she was guilty, she was convicted by manifesting certain physical symptoms (Num. 5:11–31).

The rabbis were quite uncomfortable with this trial by ordeal. The Mishnah teaches, "When adulterers increased in number, the application of the waters of jealousy ceased; and R. Jochanan ben Zakkai abolished them."[16] The Gemarah comments:

> Our Rabbis taught: "And the man shall be free from iniquity" (Num. 5:31). At the time when the man is free from iniquity, the water proves his wife; but when the man is not free from iniquity, the water

does not prove his wife. . . . Come and hear "For they themselves turn aside with whores and sacrifice with prostitutes" (Hos. 4:14). . . . R. Eliezer said: The prophet spoke to Israel. If you are scrupulous with yourselves, the water will prove your wives, otherwise the water will not prove your wives.[17]

This source is one of the earliest that expects marital fidelity from a husband as well as from a wife. The rabbis invalidated the trial by ordeal because it violated their sense of fairness. Why should a man be allowed publicly to accuse his wife of infidelity when he was free to consort with prostitutes? This passage is a step toward a single standard in the marriage relationship.

Today, we must make that equality explicit. Rabbis must stress the centrality of marital fidelity by both partners in the premarital interview. When a partner says that he or she will not remain faithful (i.e., he or she wants an open marriage), the rabbi should decline to perform the ceremony.

Perhaps equality can be built into the marriage service itself. In the traditional ceremony the groom hands his bride a ring and says, "Behold, with this ring you are *mekudeshet* (sanctified—set aside) for me according to the laws of Moses and the people Israel." Although many American rabbis use a double-ring ceremony, there is no tradition as to what the bride should say. An appropriate line might be, "Behold, with this ring you are *mekudash* (sanctified—set aside) for me in the eyes of God and the community." This wording would make explicit the Jewish expectation of marital exclusiveness.

Let us now turn to the issue of the lack of forgiveness for adultery. In biblical times, the punishment for adultery was death. To make it virtually impossible ever to put someone to death, the rabbis placed numerous restrictions on the possibility of conviction. For example, they required two witnesses to the adulterous act, proper warning, and acknowledgment of that warning. By talmudic times lashes were substituted for capital punishment.

Even two thousand years ago, Jewish leaders felt uncomfortable about judging an adulterer too harshly.

The Torah forbids the woman who commits adultery from returning to her husband. The rabbis also forbade her from her lover. If she married her lover, the rabbis could force them to divorce. Rabbinic thinking about adultery left no room for forgiveness.

In spite of the rabbinic hard line, there is ample precedent in Jewish sources for a more forgiving attitude. God tells the prophet Hosea to take a wife with a reputation for harlotry. Hosea marries Gomer and has several children, but she commits adultery. Yet in the end Hosea takes her back.

Hosea himself came to understand that his relationship with Gomer symbolized the relationship between God and the people Israel. Israel was the wife who played the harlot by worshiping idols. In the end God would take Israel back:

> Return, O Israel, to the LORD your God,
> For you have fallen because of your sin.
> Take words with you
> And return to the LORD.
> Say to Him:
> Forgive all guilt
> And accept what is good.
> . . .
> I will heal their affliction
> Generously will I take them back in love;
> For My anger has turned away from them. (Hos. 14:2–3,5)

> And I will espouse you forever:
> I will espouse you with righteousness and justice,
> And with goodness and mercy,
> And I will espouse you with faithfulness;
> Then you shall be devoted to the LORD. (Hos. 2:21–22)

The forgiving words of Hosea offer a much better paradigm for us than the punitive approach of the rabbis. Following this model, a marriage threatened by adultery can be rebuilt. It may take many years and careful counseling for the trust to be reestablished, but if God can forgive the Jews and establish His covenant with Israel forever, the marital covenant can certainly be reestablished after an indiscretion.

In my rabbinic counseling, I always try to save a marriage. Certainly the unfaithful partner must completely break off the relationship with his or her lover. The couple must pledge fidelity to each other and attempt to rebuild trust. Then they can begin anew, for central to Judaism is *teshuvah*—literally, return to the proper path. Forgiveness and rebuilding after an indiscretion are possible and desirable.

Finally, we turn to the matter of punishing the children. The Torah teaches, "Parents should not be put to death for children, nor children be put to death for parents; a person shall be put to death only for his own crime" (Deut. 24:16). In spite of this teaching, the Torah does punish the child of adultery or incest: he or she becomes a *mamzer*.

In popular terminology, *mamzer* is a derogatory term, but in actuality the term *mamzer* has to do not with one's moral character but with the facts of one's birth. According to the rabbis, it is preferable to be a *mamzer* and a scholar than the High Priest and an ignoramus.[18] A *mamzer* is a full Jew in every way but one: he or she cannot marry a Jew of legitimate birth. The children of such a marriage would also be *mamzerim*. (A *mamzer* can marry another *mamzer* or a convert to Judaism. If a *mamzer* should break the law and marry a Jew of legitimate birth, the marriage is valid after the fact.)

The issue of *mamzerut* has become even more central today with the high rate of divorce. Many Jewish women divorce their husbands civilly without obtaining a *get*, or Jewish divorce, and then remarry. Most Reform rabbis will perform such a remarriage; Conservative and Orthodox rabbis will not. Technically in Jewish law, the woman remains married to her first husband, and relations with the second husband thus constitute adultery. Any children from the second marriage are considered *mamzerim*.

The rabbis in talmudic times were troubled by the issue of *mamzerut*. They spoke of ways to purify a *mamzer*, at least in the second generation, and were willing to bend over backward to establish a presumption of legitimacy for a child. For example, when a woman gave birth after her husband had been overseas for as long as a year, the rabbis declared the child legitimate on the presumption that it was a long pregnancy.[19] They were willing to ignore biological facts to preserve the legitimacy and marriageability of a child.

This attitude gives us some insight on how to deal with the issue of *mamzerut* today. There must be a presumption of legitimacy for every Jew. Although the laws of *mamzerut* can remain on the books, they should not be applied in practice. There is clear precedent for such an approach. The Torah speaks of a stubborn and rebellious son who can be put to death by his parents (Deut. 21:18–21). The rabbis later declared, "There never was and there never will be a stubborn and rebellious son. Why is it in the Torah? So we can study it and receive a reward."[20]

Similarly, we can restrict the laws of *mamzerut* to be a subject for theoretical study. In reality, this is precisely what usually happens today. Orthodox rabbis will try to find some technical problem in the first marriage to remove the requirement for a *get* and the stigma of *mamzerut*. Conservative rabbis will ignore the issue and perform the wedding of a *mamzer* with a legitimate Jew, since under Jewish law the marriage is legitimate after the fact. Reform rabbis have removed the category of *mamzer* along with all other biological categories such as Kohen and Levi. Each movement in its own way has thus removed *mamzerut* as a practical issue; each is disturbed by the traditional practice of punishing children for the sins of their parents.

Finally, let us turn to a difficult question. We have already established that the essence of marriage is an exclusive sexual relationship. What about the case in which one partner in a marriage is
incapacitated and unable to have sex? Is the other partner permitted to take a lover for sexual fulfillment, or must he or she first
seek a divorce? Is someone who wishes to remain married out of
love or loyalty to a lifelong spouse condemned to a life of celibacy?

This situation is sad but not unusual. Often one partner is
physically or mentally unable to have sex, leaving the other partner
sexually frustrated. Although Jewish sources permit divorce in
such a case, this option is often neither emotionally nor financially
feasible. On the other hand, no Jewish source gives permission for
adultery, no matter how tragic the circumstances. Judaism teaches
that marital fidelity is an absolute, and any compromise in that
stand would open up a Pandora's box of abuse.

Nevertheless, there is room for compassion and understanding toward a married individual who ignores the law and becomes
involved in an adulterous relationship. We must apply the Sage
Hillel's famous dictum, "Do not judge another until you stand in
his place."[21]

Much can be learned by studying the precedent of Lot and his
daughters (Gen. 19:30–37). Although incest is condemned as a
fundamental sin in the Torah, both Lot's daughters commit incest
with their father after the destruction of Sodom. They mistakenly
believe that they are the last people on earth. The midrash takes
into account the extenuating circumstances and avoids condemning their actions.

CONCLUSIONS

Judaism recognizes that in certain situations the sex act can
hurt and destroy. Immoral sex includes sex based on lies and

deceit, insensitive comments about a partner's sexual ability, and serious transgressions such as rape, incest, and adultery.

Judaism teaches that we human beings are not mere animals, subject to blind urges and instincts. Rather, we have the ability to control our sexual drive. Rabbi Maurice Lamm writes:

> How can we control seemingly autonomous feelings? Ibn Ezra answers that we have to train ourselves to understand that certain objects of desire are impossible to achieve—that which we can never hope to attain cannot be the object of our dreams. We must rule them out of the framework of our reality because of our fear of God.[22]

We are in control, not our drives and desires.

Immoral sex is an unfortunate fact of modern life. Children grow up as victims of sexual abuse. Women are victims of rape by acquaintances as well as strangers. Even the best marriages can be threatened by an indiscretion. The question for the Jewish community is how to rebuild from the ruins of sexual immorality. How can victims of rape or incest rebuild their self-esteem? How can marriages damaged by adultery rebuild trust and love? In ages past, the issue was the kind of sexual activity that was forbidden. For our modern society, the issue is *teshuvah* (return), finding the way back to oneness with self, family, spouse, and God after forbidden sex.

4

Is LIVING TOGETHER IMMORAL?

> What is the difference between a wife and a concubine?
> R. Judah said in the name of Rav: A wife has a
> *ketubbah* and *kiddushin*, a concubine has neither.
>
> *Sanhedrin 21a*

THE MAN was in his late forties, as was his woman friend. Both divorced, they shared an apartment and were active in Jewish life. In a lighter moment, I hinted that perhaps I ought to make their living arrangement legal. The man answered, "Rabbi, we both have tried marriage. It didn't work for us. We are both happy with our current arrangement, but if we ever change our mind, we'll call you."

Judaism may see marriage as the ideal, but adults today seem to be spending less and less of their adult life married. They are marrying later or perhaps not at all, divorcing at an alarming rate, and becoming widowed at an age when they can still be sexually active. Birth control devices and cures for venereal disease have removed the two basic fears of sex outside marriage. (In recent years, the AIDS epidemic has revived some of these fears.) Sex outside of marriage has become so common that adults almost take it for granted.

Popular culture has reinforced this casual acceptance of sex outside of marriage. Rare is the movie or popular novel that does not have the obligatory bedroom scene. At one time remaining a virgin until marriage was a source of pride; today it is usually a source of embarrassment. Contemporary etiquette concerns itself not with whether to sleep together before marriage, but at what point—after one date, three dates, or only after engagement. To wait until marriage is no longer fashionable.

This chapter explores the issue of nonmarital sex,[1] that is, sexual relations between *unmarried, consenting adults*. Each of these three words is important. If one of the adults is married, the relationship becomes adulterous. If one of the adults is nonconsenting, it is a case of rape. If one of the partners is not an adult (eighteen or older), the relationship involves another dimension—teenage sex—which I examine more closely in chapter 9. Unmarried, consenting adults may be casual acquaintances, lovers, or an engaged couple.

The issue of nonmarital sex is quite complicated, as Ruth Westheimer and Louis Lieberman explain in their recent book on sexual morality:

> Of all the issues we examine in this book, the question of whether or not to engage in some form of sexual activity before, instead of or after marriage is the most complex one in terms of moral standards. This is due to the very confusing set of sexual standards that has developed as part of the culture of the people instead of as a moral code that emanates from religion. For example, there are unmarried young women we know of who believe it is O.K. to have coital sex with someone they love but not with someone they do not love. There are others who believe that they can honestly present themselves as virgins to a prospective mate if they are "technical virgins," that is, they may have had all kinds of oral, anal and manual sex, sometimes with many partners, but without vaginal penetration.[2]

The question for unmarried adults is not simply whether or not to have sex but what types of sexual activities are appropriate at what stage in a relationship.

MODERN RABBINIC VIEWS OF NONMARITAL SEX

It is common knowledge that Jewish law forbids sexual relations outside the context of marriage. Numerous rabbis from all the movements have written that marriage is the only proper forum for relations. A sampling of opinions from a number of contemporary rabbis follows.

David Feldman, a Conservative rabbi, writes:

Marriage is an institution to protect the partners from the uncertainties of changing moods and the lure of competing claims on their affections. Marriage thus prevents the ultimate human relationship from being trivialized; it does the same for sex itself. The holy and essentially human character of the sexual relationship obtains when the sexual is part of an umbrella of relationships—physical, emotional, social. Being the most intimate, the sexual is reserved for the most total of relationships.[3]

A leading Conservative thinker, Professor Robert Gordis, writes:

Far from strengthening the institution of marriage, a premarital relationship undermines it at its most basic. If marriage is to survive in spite of all its liabilities, it must be endowed with one unique attribute characteristic of it and of it alone—*it must be the only theater for experiencing the most intimate interplay of love and sex.* [Emphasis in original.] Marriage must have this special quality in order to survive the limitless challenges and temptations of modern life in a free and open society.[4]

Eugene B. Borowitz, a noted Reform theologian, writes:

The most ethical form of human relationship I know is love-for-life. Its appropriate social and religious structure is the monogamous marriage. This being so, marriage is, if I may use the strange formulation of ethical pluralism, the most right context, that is, the best criterion for the validity of sexual intercourse. And I think every human being should try to reach the highest possible level of ethical behavior.[5]

Maurice Lamm, a leading Orthodox rabbi, writes:

> In the Jewish view, it is insufficient to affirm that the act must have meaning: it must also have value. For Judaism, value in human sexuality comes only when the relationship involves two people who have committed themselves to one another and have made that commitment in a binding covenant recognized by God and by society. The act of sexual union, the deepest personal statement that any human being can make, must be reserved for the moment of total oneness.
>
> The sexual act is the first and most significant event of married life, and its force and beauty should not be compromised by sharing coitus in the expectation that some day a decision will be made to marry or not marry. The act of sex is not only a declaration of present love, it is a covenantal statement of permanent commitment. It is only in this frame of reference that sexual congress is legitimate, because only then is it a religious act, a de'var mitzvah.[6]

Such unanimity, rare enough among the various movements, suggests that the matter is an open-and-shut case. Is this rabbinic consensus realistic, however? Can we expect our young people to avoid sexual relations until marriage when many do not marry until their twenties or thirties, if at all? Can we expect couples after divorce to return to a life of celibacy until they find a new marriage partner? Even if we maintain that nonmarital sex is forbidden, how do we view the majority of Jews who will not or cannot live up to this standard? Are they to be condemned? Does Jewish tradition allow any flexibility on this matter?

Let us turn to the issue of nonmarital sex as it is presented in the Torah and developed in rabbinic literature. The results are surprising.

EXPLORING JEWISH SOURCES

The written Torah never forbids sex outside the context of marriage, with the exception of adultery and incest. On the contrary, the Torah seems to assume that it is a natural part of life. For example, when Judah sleeps with his daughter-in-law Tamar, mistaking her for a prostitute (Gen. 38), he is never condemned for the sexual act, only for avoiding his levirate responsibilities. Similarly, when King David in his old age is unable to keep warm, a young virgin, Abishag the Shunammite, is brought to share his bed and wait on him (1 Kings 1:1–4). The Bible is natural and unembarrassed about the sexual activities of its major personalities. Although adultery and incest are explicitly forbidden, fornication is not.

The Torah is concerned primarily about what the loss of virginity might mean to a young woman of marriageable age. Two laws, one concerning seduction and the other concerning rape, explicitly spell out this concern:

> If a man seduces a virgin for whom the bride price has not been paid, and lies with her, he must make her his wife by payment of a bride price. If her father refuses to give her to him, he must still weigh out silver in accordance with the bride price of virgins. (Exod. 22:15–16)

> If a man comes upon a virgin who is not engaged and he seizes her and lies with her, and they are discovered, the man who lay with her shall pay the girl's father fifty [shekels of] silver, and she shall be his wife. Because he has violated her, he can never have the right to divorce her. (Deut. 22:28–29)

Raping or seducing a young woman meant a financial loss to her family; therefore a fine had to be paid. Also, given the vital status of a bride's virginity in the biblical world, loss of virginity would likely minimize her ability to find a husband. Therefore, the seducer is forced to marry her and loses the automatic right of divorce usually given to a man.[7]

In spite of these two laws, virginity for its own sake has never been a Jewish ideal. The Bible tells the tragic story of Jephthah, forced to sacrifice his daughter because of an ill-conceived vow. Before her untimely death, Jephthah's daughter goes for two months into the hills to bewail her virginity (Judg. 11). In contrast to Christianity, which regarded lifelong virginity as a sign of piety, Judaism has viewed it as a tragedy.

In rabbinic law, a woman's virginity has certain financial consequences at the time of marriage. If the bride is a virgin, the *ketubbah* paid by the husband is two hundred *zuz*; if she is not a virgin, it is one hundred *zuz*.[8] A man's virginity is never discussed. An unmarried woman who chooses to have sex with an unmarried man and is willing to live with the financial consequences has not broken any explicit law of the Torah. In fact, in Judah the established custom was for betrothed couples to have sexual relations before marriage.[9]

It was the rabbis of the talmudic period who explicitly outlawed nonmarital sexual relations. One fascinating passage articulates the rabbinic attitude:

> Rab Judah said in Rab's name: A man once conceived a passion for a certain woman, and his heart was consumed by his burning desire [his life being endangered thereby]. When the doctors were consulted, they said: "His only cure is that she shall submit." Thereupon the sages said: "Let him die rather than that she should yield." Then [doctors said]: "Let her stand nude before him." [The sages answered]: "Sooner he should die." The doctors said: "Let her converse with him from behind the fence." "Let him die," the sages replied, "rather than that she should converse with him from behind a fence."
>
> Now R. Jacob b. Idi and R. Samuel b. Nahmani dispute therein. One said that she was a married woman, the other that she was unmarried. Now, this is intelligible on the view that she was a married woman, but on the latter, that she was unmarried, why such severity? R. Papa said: Because of the disgrace to her family. R. Aha the son of R. Ika said: That the daughters of Israel not be immorally dissolute.
>
> Then why not marry her? Marriage would not assuage his passion, even as R. Isaac said: Since the destruction of the Temple, sexual pleasure has been taken [from those who practice it lawfully] and given to sinners, as it is written: "Stolen waters are sweet and bread eaten in secret is pleasant" (Prov. 9:17).[10]

The rabbis forbid this man to have sexual relations or even converse in private with this woman even though she is single and doing so would save his life. They give two reasons: protecting her family name and preventing the daughters of Israel from being morally dissolute. We see here evidence of a rabbinic morality which has developed beyond strict biblical law.

A number of rabbinic laws and practices attempted to reinforce the new attitude toward nonmarital sex. Most important was promoting the ideal of marriage at a young age. A father was expected to arrange a marriage for his daughter while she was still a *na'arah*, a young maiden between twelve and twelve and one-half years old.[11] Beyond that age she was no longer in the father's control; the husband could no longer make the legal claim that his wife was not a virgin. The ideal age of marriage for a young man was eighteen. According to the Talmud, the younger, the better:

> A man who is twenty and unmarried lives all his days in sin. Do you really mean "in sin"? Rather say "in thoughts of sin". Rava taught and some say the school of Ishmael taught: "Until the age of twenty the Holy One, Blessed be He, waits to see when he will marry. Upon reaching twenty and not marrying, He says, 'Blast his bones.' "
> R. Hisda taught: "I am preferable to my colleagues because I married at sixteen. Had I married at fourteen, I could have said to the satan: 'An arrow in your eye.' "[12]

To the rabbis, early marriage was the best way to control the sexual drive and prevent premarital sex. To this day arranged marriages at a very young age are still the practice in hasidic and other ultra-Orthodox communities.

The rabbis took other measures to prevent sexual relations outside the sanctity of marriage. For example, by Torah law a man could acquire a wife by cohabiting with her for purposes of marriage. The Mishnah teaches, "A woman is acquired [as a wife] in three ways. . . . By money, by a document, and by sexual intercourse."[13] However, the rabbis ruled that such a practice was against Jewish morality: "Rav punished any man who betrothed a woman . . . with intercourse."[14]

Nevertheless, the rabbis established the presumption that a man does not simply have intercourse for purposes of promiscuity.[15] If a man and woman have slept together, the rabbis ruled that there must have been marital intent. Thus, even in talmudic times, Judaism recognized the reality of common-law marriage.[16]

Although common-law marriage may be recognized after the fact, rabbinic law prohibited sexual relations between a man and his betrothed. (Betrothal, the first in two steps in establishing a Jewish marriage, used to take place a year before the actual marriage. Today betrothal and marriage have been joined together in one ceremony.) This law led to the establishment of the *birkat eirusin*, the only blessing in Jewish tradition over a forbidden activity:

> Praised are You, Lord our God, King of the universe, who has sanctified us with His commandments and commanded us regarding forbidden relations, forbidding sexual relations with our betrothed, permitting marital relations following *huppah* and *kiddushin*. Praised are You, who sanctifies His people Israel by *huppah* and *kiddushin*.

This blessing, chanted today over a cup of wine at the beginning of the wedding ceremony, states explicitly that holiness is achieved by avoiding improper sexual relationships and establishing proper ones.

The rabbis of the talmudic era also laid down strict rulings regarding modesty and the separation of the sexes. The intermingling of the sexes in public, even in synagogue, was frowned upon. A man and a woman unrelated by blood or marriage were not permitted *yihud*, being alone together in private. Louis Epstein, whose *Sex Laws and Customs in Judaism* is the classic work on this subject, writes about the early talmudic period:

> One of the leading principles of the Men of the Great Synagogue, the religious teachers of the early part of that period, was "Make a fence

about the law" (Avot 1:1), so that by respecting the "fence" one would avoid transgressing the law itself. In the chain of tradition, as the Men of the Great Synagogue handed the law down to the Hasmonean court and they in turn to their pharisaic successors, a considerable number of restrictions beyond the requirement of the original law, called takkanot and gezerot, were enacted and added to the law as "fences" or safeguards.

This process had a significant effect upon the code of sex morality. Nowhere is a fence needed so much as in the control of sex passions. This period, therefore, distinguished itself by unnumbered restrictions against social contact between men and women, against sitting alongside a woman at a festive table, against drinking a cup of wine with her at a social gathering, even against speaking to a woman or gazing upon her. The separation of the sexes was thoroughgoing enough, but should an occasion arise when a man and a woman were thrown into each other's company, it was required that a chaperone be present.[17]

Part of what separates the liberal Orthodox from the more insular Orthodox communities is the strictness with which they follow these laws. Among the more liberal Conservative and Reform movements, these "fences" have fallen by the wayside.

Through such rulings and teachings, the rabbis attempted to prevent Jews from participating in nonmarital sexual relations. However, they could not unequivocally claim that nonmarital sex was forbidden in the Torah. Only one rabbi tried to find a Torah basis for the prohibition:

> "Do not degrade your daughter and make her a harlot, lest the land fall into harlotry and the land be filled with depravity" (Lev. 19:29). R. Eliezer taught: this refers to an unmarried man who comes upon an unmarried woman not for purposes of marriage.[18]

Rabbi Eliezer's ruling was not accepted as the halakhah. After all, the Torah does permit a man to take a concubine, that is, a woman in a monogamous sexual relationship without a ketubbah or the traditional kiddushin.[19]

Maimonides, in his great code of Jewish law, the *Mishnah Torah*, follows Rabbi Eliezer's lead in outlawing all nonmarital sexual relations. Before the giving of the Torah, he writes, a man would meet a woman in the marketplace, take her home, and she would become his wife. Or he would meet a woman, pay her a fee, and have a sexual encounter with her. Since the giving of the Torah, however, prostitution has become forbidden and marriage now requires a public ceremony including *ketubbah* and *kiddushin* before witnesses. Any other sexual encounter is akin to prostitution, which is forbidden by the Torah.[20]

Maimonides' ruling is not universally accepted. The Ravad (Rabbi Avraham ben David) criticizes the Rambam: "Prostitution is only when she is promiscuous and sleeps with any man, but if she is set aside for one man there is no prohibition. This is the concubine discussed in the Torah."[21]

To summarize, the accepted position in Judaism by rabbis of all movements is that nonmarital sex is forbidden. However, as we have seen, this position is not without controversy. The Torah never explicitly forbids nonmarital sex. In fact, it permits the taking of a concubine, a woman who has an exclusive relationship with a man without *kiddushin* or *ketubbah*, the basic necessities of marriage.[22] In other words, it is parallel to our modern living together without benefit of clergy. Eventually concubinage fell out of usage in the Jewish community.

At least one eighteenth-century scholar, Rabbi Jacob Emden, sought to reintroduce the institution of the concubine into his community. In a long, technical responsum, Rabbi Emden writes that concubinage may be a solution to the sexual immorality of his own day:

> [Some say] the Ramban who permits a concubine, in our day when men are morally lax, sleeping with maid servants and forbidden sexual partners, would forbid it. . . . It seems to me the opposite. For this reason the master would permit it, so that people would not commit

greater offenses involving karet (excision) from the Torah. For a man with bread in his basket will not have the same burning desire to go after forbidden relations. There are similar rulings where the rabbis have permitted even something forbidden by rabbinic law to prevent a Torah transgression.[23]

Emden's ruling was hardly liberal by modern standards of sexual practice. He insists that the couple observe the laws of family purity, remain absolutely faithful to one another, and enter such a relationship only in consultation with a rabbi. Even with these restrictions, Emden realized that he was proposing something radical. He ends his responsum with a referral to the rabbinic principle that "when it is time to work for the Lord, they may change Thy Torah," which was sometimes used by the rabbis to overturn a law in the Torah.[24]

Emden was deeply concerned about the sexual immorality in his day and was therefore willing to propose such a radical solution. He was acting upon the principle that it is better for people to engage in sexual activity that has some degree of religious sanction than in totally forbidden activity. Emden's proposal is analogous to the ladder of holiness concept proposed in chapter 2. Although living together outside marriage does not possess the same level of legitimacy as marriage, it is far better than the promiscuity prevalent in Emden's day.

Still, most rabbis and the Jewish community as a whole rejected Emden's proposal. The day of the concubine had passed from Jewish life. From then on sex would be permissible only within the context of marriage. Any other form of sexual activity fell short of the rabbinic vision of holiness.

CONCLUSIONS FOR MODERN JEWS

As we have seen, the Torah never explicitly outlaws nonmarital sex (except in the case of adultery and incest); it was the rabbis who later forbade it. Even when there was room for a more liberal sexual morality, the rabbis refused to be permissive. Sex outside marriage simply did not fit their ideal of holiness. Why did the rabbis take such a hard line?

I argue that the rabbis were trying to protect the institution of marriage. To them marriage was not simply one of many life-style options; it was the ideal way to live. "A man who does not have a wife lives without joy, without blessing, and without goodness."[25] They understood only too well the dangers of nonmarital sex. Why search for a mate when it is far easier to search for a sexual partner? Why bother to stay faithful within marriage when one has been sexually promiscuous before marriage? Our modern experience seems to prove a correlation between loose sexual morality before marriage and weak marriages.

One young Orthodox rabbi has written clearly on this point:

> It is no longer clear to me that single adulthood in and of itself is responsible for the relaxed sexual morality of our generation. The reverse is true as well. Free sex encourages a casual attitude toward relationships generally, which, in turn, further discourages early marriages. The prevailing cultural prejudice that marriage is not necessary, and that a young couple ought to live together for a considerable time before considering marriage, discouraged me, for example, from cultivating relationships with those women who still adhered to the "outmoded" norm of premarital chastity. Furthermore, I found that this attitude encourages predatory and exploitative approaches toward sexual partners, particularly on the part of men.[26]

As we saw, the rabbis refused to allow a man to have sexual relations with a woman even when it would save his life because such relations would set a poor example for the daughters of Israel. In general, the rabbis taught that condoning permissive sexual behavior undermines the marriage ideal that they were attempting to protect.

The rabbis had certain secondary concerns when they outlawed nonmarital sex. For example, an unmarried woman would be embarrassed to go to the *mikvah* and therefore could not properly maintain the laws of family purity. Today an issue in some Orthodox circles is whether it is permissible for a sexually active unmarried woman to go to the *mikvah* each month. Another concern of the rabbis was the lineage of children born from casual sexual encounters. Rabbi Eliezer, the only Mishnaic rabbi explicitly to outlaw nonmarital sex, wrote:

> He sleeps with many women and he does not know who they all are. She receives many men and does not know who she receives. It will turn out that a man will err and marry his sister, a woman will err and marry her brother and the world will be filled with mamzerim.[27]

Jacob Emden, when he permits concubinage, insists that a woman wait three months after leaving such a relationship before marrying to ascertain the lineage of children.

These issues, although important, are still only secondary. The rabbis outlawed nonmarital sex primarily because of its potential to undermine marriage. If ultimate fulfillment was to come only within marriage, then any sexual relationship short of marriage could be used as an excuse for avoiding marital commitment. If holiness was to be the Jewish ideal, then every effort had to be made to sanctify sex by limiting it to the ideal relationship.

These concerns are as valid today as they were in talmudic times. The Jewish community still seeks to encourage marriage as an ideal and discourage any behavior that might undermine marriage. Perhaps not every Jew lives up to the ideal; in fact, today only a small minority maintains the ideal of chastity before marriage and fidelity within marriage. Nevertheless, it is possible—perhaps even imperative—to establish and uphold an ideal even if few Jews live up to it.

The Jewish community can adopt policies which promote this ideal, as a simple example from my own synagogue illustrates. A couple living together but unmarried applied to become members. After much discussion, we decided that they could join as two singles but not as one family. We felt that the synagogue's membership policy should reflect the ideals of Judaism.

In a similar way, I have argued for the right of parents to insist that an unmarried child and a boyfriend or girlfriend have separate bedrooms when coming to visit. Children have told me, "Rabbi, it's hypocritical. We sleep together in college. Why shouldn't we sleep together when we come home to visit my parents?" My answer is that parents have a right to set values for their own household.

Given the widespread practice of premarital sex, many have questioned the wording of the traditional *ketubbah* (marriage document), which mentions the virginal status of the bride and its financial consequences. A virgin bride has a *ketubbah* of two hundred *zuz*; a widow, divorcee, or convert has a *ketubbah* of one hundred *zuz*. The general practice among Conservative and Orthodox Jews is to write *betultah* (virgin) even when the word does not fit the facts. (The Reform movement has rewritten the *ketubbah* in an egalitarian style, omitting all mention of the bride's status and all financial consequences.) Many protest that the traditional language often builds a lie into the marriage ceremony.

Rabbi Robert Gordis has called for a reworking of the traditional *ketubbah*, replacing *betultah* with the word *panyetah* (single, unmarried).[28] He claims that there is precedent in ancient *genizah* manuscripts for such a change. Gordis writes, "By reviving this usage of a millennium ago, we shall obviate any possible stigma or embarrassment to the parties concerned and at the same time obey the biblical injunction, 'Love peace and truth' (Zecharia 8:19)."[29]

The majority of rabbis have not accepted Gordis's suggestion for two reasons. First, the term *betultah* was never meant as a physiological description of the bride, but rather as a description of her legal status. The Talmud already provides a precedent for using *betultah* to refer to a woman who is not technically a virgin but has the legal status and the financial rights of a woman not previously married.[30]

A second reason to retain the traditional wording is that to change it is to give up on an ideal that Jews have tried to maintain for thousands of years. Such a change would serve as a public statement that the majority of Jewish brides are no longer virgins. Today many women and men, not just in the Orthodox community, maintain the Jewish ideal of premarital virginity. Even if the majority of Jews do not, it is legitimate to maintain the legal fiction that they do. Such a statement upholds an ideal of holiness before the Jewish community.

Similarly, rabbis should continue to preach the Jewish ideal of premarital chastity. In their own personal behavior, rabbis and other communal leaders who are single should be above reproach. Rabbis should take this stand *not* because nonmarital sex is immoral or unethical, but because it falls short of the holiness ideal carefully crafted by the Torah and the Talmud.

While taking a public stand on behalf of sex within marriage, rabbis and communal leaders must also recognize that many if not most Jews may not live up to this ideal. A rabbi called upon to counsel an unmarried person on sexual matters must do so with sensitivity and compassion, not judgment. A teaching of Rabbi Ilai the elder is useful:

> If a man sees that his Evil Impulse is conquering him, he should go to a place where he is unknown, put on black clothes, wrap himself in a black cloak, and do what his heart desires, but let him not publicly profane the name of heaven.[31]

The wisdom of Rabbi Ilai is that he acknowledges the reality of improper sexual behavior; he does not condemn it but instead takes precautions to prevent it from becoming the norm. In ancient times and in our own, there is an ideal to strive for in our sexual conduct. It behooves the Jewish community publicly to maintain that ideal.

5

THE MARITAL BEDROOM

When there is no union of male and female, men are
not worthy of beholding the Divine Presence.
                    Zohar, vol. 3, Aharei Mot 59a

JUDAISM TEACHES that sex reaches the highest level of
holiness within the context of marriage. Many rabbinic passages
suggest that God's presence dwells only where a husband and wife
dwell together. Holiness can be found as readily in the marital
bedroom as in the synagogue. Therefore, the rabbis teach that to
live without a spouse is to live without joy, blessing, or goodness.[1]
In Hebrew, a bachelor is a *ravak*, from a root meaning "empty."

Marriage demands an exclusive sexual relationship. Just as sex
without marriage is not consistent with the Jewish holiness ideal,
so marriage without sex is not truly a marriage. Platonic marriages,
considered the ideal in some Christian sources, have no place in
Judaism. The Talmud, after discussing whether a couple can make
a prenuptial agreement to avoid sexual relations in their marriage,
concludes that such an agreement is prohibited, although almost
any financial prenuptial arrangement is permitted.[2]

In Jewish marriage, sex has two purposes. The secondary purpose is procreation (see chapter 6); the primary purpose is companionship and self-fulfillment. When the Torah establishes marriage
as an institution, it never mentions children. At the beginning of
Genesis, the Torah declares, "It is not good for man to be alone;

I will make a fitting helper for him. . . . Hence a man leaves his father and mother and clings to his wife, so that they become one flesh" (Gen. 2:18, 24). Thus even people unable to have children because of infertility or menopause find the ideal life within marriage and regular sexual relations.

Nevertheless, not all sexual activity is permissible or desirable within marriage. Numerous sources define the Jewish ideal in marital sex, and the rabbis were quite open in their discussion of many sexual topics, including frequency, positions, foreplay, women's orgasms, sexual fantasy, and modesty. Most important, marital sex ought to be built on a foundation of love, communication, and mutual respect between husband and wife.

THE LAWS OF MARITAL SEX[3]

Jewish law mandates that sex between husband and wife take place on a regular basis. This law is called *onah* and derives from the Biblical verse: ". . . he must not withhold from this one her food, her clothing, or her conjugal rights (*onatah*)" (Exod. 21:10). Although this passage refers specifically to a slave girl, the rabbis expanded upon it to include relations between husband and wife.

The word *onatah* literally means "her time" and refers to the right of a woman to regular intercourse. In Judaism, regular sex is *a woman's right and a man's duty*. This attitude stands precisely opposite the norm in Western culture, in which we often speak of a man's right and a woman's duty. From the beginning Judaism has recognized that women have sexual needs and that men have a responsibility to fulfill them. Within the tradition, avoiding the marital responsibility is considered *tzarah de-gufah*, a "hardship for the body" of the woman.[4]

The Talmud defines precisely the requirement of *onah*. The question is raised: for how long can a man take a vow of sexual abstinence?

If one put his wife under a vow to have no sexual intercourse, the School of Shammai says for two weeks, but the School of Hillel says for one week. Disciples may go forth to the study of Torah without permission for thirty days, laborers for one week. The times for onah as enjoined in the law are: for men of independent means every day, for workmen twice weekly, for ass drivers once a week, for camel drivers once every thirty days, for sailors once every six months. This is the opinion of R. Eliezer.[5]

The Talmud adds that it is a particular mitzvah for scholars to have intercourse on Friday night, thus joining the holiness of the Sabbath with the holiness of marital sex. The rabbis put a clear limit on how long a man can avoid his marital duty by a vow, by going off to study, or for professional reasons. The numbers represent a minimum; a husband is obliged to initiate sex with his wife whenever she desires it, even beyond the obligation of onah.[6]

If a man wishes to change his profession to one which would make him less available for the mitzvah of onah (for example, from an ass driver to a camel driver), he must receive permission from his wife. The Talmud teaches that "a woman would rather have one bushel and her husband's presence than ten bushels and separation."[7] From this example we learn a lesson relevant to couples today who consider changing jobs with the result that they will be less available for one another. Based on this rabbinic teaching, a woman could say to her husband, "I would rather that you did not travel in order to be more available for me, even if it means having less money." A man could say the same to his wife.

The mitzvah of onah is not simply a negative commandment not to withhold sexual relations. The rabbis also saw it as the positive commandment of simḥat ishto, rejoicing in one's wife, a notion based upon a verse in the Torah: "When a man has taken a bride, he shall not go out with the army or be assigned to it for any purpose; he shall be exempt one year for the sake of his household, to give happiness to the woman he has married" (Deut.

24:5). The Talmud interprets this verse as follows: "A man is required to give joy to his wife in the matter of the mitzvah."[8]

Simply performing one's marital duty pro forma is not in keeping with the Jewish ideal. The Torah requires joy, frivolity, even spontaneity in the sexual relations between husband and wife. The Torah describes the sex life between Isaac and his wife Rebekah with the term *metzaḥeik*, "to make laugh" (Gen. 26:8). Both husband and wife should maximize their pleasure in the sexual act. *Iggeret ha-Kodesh*, the Epistle of Holiness, often attributed to Nachmanides, has a section called "On the Quality of the Act":

> Therefore, when engaging in the sex act, you must begin by speaking to her in a manner that will draw her heart to you, calm her spirits, and make her happy. Speak to her so that your words will provoke desire, love, will, and passion, as well as words leading to reverence for God, piety, and modesty. Tell her how pious and modest women are blessed with upright, honorable, and worthy children. . . . Therefore a husband should speak with his wife with appropriate words, some of erotic passion, some words of fear of the Lord.
>
> A man should never force himself upon his wife and never overpower her, for the Divine Spirit never rests upon one whose conjugal relations occur in the absence of desire, love and free will. The Shekhinah does not rest there. One should never argue with his wife, and certainly never strike her on account of sexual matters. The Talmud tells us that just as a lion tears at his prey and eats it shamelessly, so does an ignorant man shamelessly strike and sleep with his wife (Pesakhim 49b). Rather act so that you will warm her heart by speaking to her charming and seductive words.
>
> To conclude, when you are ready for sexual union, see that your wife's intentions combine with yours. Do not hurry to arouse her until she is receptive. Be calm, and as you enter the path of love and will, let her insemination come first. . . .[9]

The last line of the quotation goes beyond foreplay, loving conversation, and arousal of the woman to demonstrate a concern for a woman's orgasm a thousand years before such matters became a fashionable topic of conversation and concern. The Talmud, a far earlier source, already speaks of the importance of women's orgasms:

> What is exactly meant by "The fruit of the womb, His reward" (Ps. 127:3)? R. Hama son of R. Hanina replied: As a reward for containing oneself during intercourse in the womb, in order that one's wife emit seed first, the Holy One, Blessed be He, gives one the reward of the fruit of the womb.[10]

Other sources also speak about a woman's sexual fulfillment. For example, the Torah teaches, "When a woman brings forth seed (*tazriya*) and has a male child" (Lev. 12:2). The rabbis interpret this verse to mean that if a woman brings forth seed first—i.e., has an orgasm first—a male child will be born, an extremely desirable event. To quote the full talmudic passage:

> Rabbi Isaac, citing Rabbi Ammi, stated: If the man emits his semen first she bears a female child; for it is said: "When a woman brings forth seed and has a male child" (Lev. 12:2). Our rabbis taught: At first it used to be said that if the woman emits her semen first she will bear a male, and if the man emits his semen first she will bear a female, but the sages did not explain the reason until Rabbi Zadok came and explained it: "These were the sons whom Leah bore to Jacob in Paddan-aram, in addition to his daughter Dinah" (Gen. 46:15). Scripture thus ascribes the males to the females and the females to the males.
>
> "The descendants of Ulam—men of substance, who drew the bow, had many sons and grandsons" (1 Chron. 8:40). Now is it within the power of a man to increase the number of sons and grandsons? But the fact is that because they contained themselves during intercourse, in order that their wives should emit their semen first, so that their children shall be males, Scripture attributes to them the same merit as if they had themselves caused the increase of the number of their sons and sons' sons. This explains what Rabbi Kattina said: "I can make all my children to be males."[11]

Scientific veracity aside, this entire passage can be read as a concern for a woman's orgasm.

Judaism obligates a man to be concerned with his wife's pleasure. This concern ought to include words of endearment, proper
foreplay, a responsibility to help his wife achieve orgasm, and
postcoital intimacy. Because *onah* becomes a responsibility whenever the wife wishes it, a husband must always be aware of his
wife's sexual needs and desires. Communication therefore is vital.
A man who uses his wife to fulfill his own orgasmic needs while
leaving her unsatisfied is not fulfilling his Jewish obligations.

A woman also has a responsibility for her husband's sexual
pleasure. In an enigmatic passage in the Talmud, Rabbi Hisda
advises his daughters on how to intensify their husbands' pleasure:
"He held a jewel in one hand and a clump of soil in the other. He
showed them the jewel but did not show them the clump until they
were suffering. Then he showed them."[12] Rashi explains that the
jewel represents the breasts, and the clump of soil, the vagina.

> When your husband has marital relations and holds you with one
> hand on the breasts and the other hand on "that place" for your
> pleasure, show him your breasts to increase his appetite but do not
> show him your vagina quickly so his appetite and desire will increase.
> When he is in pain, show him.[13]

In other words, a woman should delay penetration until her husband's desire is at a maximum.

Although it is a man's duty to engage in regular sexual relations, a woman must make herself available to her husband for
those relations. Even though a man cannot force himself on his
wife, neither can a wife refuse her husband's sexual advances:

> Rami b. Hama citing R. Assi further ruled, a man is forbidden to
> compel his wife to the [marital] obligation. . . . R. Joshua b. Levi
> similarly stated: Whosoever compels his wife to the [marital] obliga-
> tion will have unworthy children.[14]

A woman is equally responsible for sexual relations in a marriage. A wife who consistently refuses her husband's sexual ad-

vances is called a *moredet*, "a rebellious wife." The Mishnah prescribes a punishment for her:

> If a woman is rebellious against her husband, he may reduce her ketubbah seven dinars every week. R. Judah says, seven half dinars. How long is the reduction to be continued? Until it reaches the full amount of her ketubbah. R. Jose says: He may continue to diminish it, in case an inheritance may fall to her from some source and he can then claim from her. And likewise also if a man rebels against his wife they may add to her marriage settlement three dinars a week. R. Jose says, three half dinars.[15]

Thus both the wife and husband can be declared rebellious by the refusal to participate in regular sexual relations. Significantly, the financial penalties are more severe for the rebellious wife. The rabbis explained that a man's sexual drive is stronger and thus his pain greater. They point out, "Observe the brothel; who pays whom?"[16]

Several generations later the rabbis modified the law of the rebellious wife:

> What is to be understood by [the term] rebellious wife? Amemar said, She who says, "I wish to remain married to him but I want to cause him pain." However if she says, "He is repulsive to me," she is not forced [to have sexual relations].
>
> Mar Zutra said, she is forced. Such an incident once occurred and Mar Zutra forced [the woman to remain married and have relations] and R. Haninah of Sura was born. This, however, was not proper. In that case, it was God's intervention that brought the positive result.[17]

This fascinating exchange is quite relevant for modern marriages. On the one hand, no woman should be forced to have sex with her husband if she finds him repulsive. On the other hand, a man or woman should not withhold sex, using it as a weapon in a fight. In my own counseling I always recommend that, when a husband and wife fight, they make every effort not to go to bed angry. The marital bed is a place of holiness, not a battleground.

The rabbinic requirement of regular sexual relations in a marriage does put some responsibility on the wife. It is considered desirable for her to solicit her husband to the sexual act. (Nevertheless, the laws of modesty suggest that she be a bit less brazen and more subtle than her husband.) "R. Samuel b. Nahmani, citing R. Johanan, stated: A woman who solicits her husband to the [marital] obligation will have children the like of whom did not exist even in the generation of Moses."[18]

Jewish law is concerned not only with the frequency of the sexual act but with the manner in which it is performed. The Talmud recommends nudity:

> R. Joseph taught: "Her flesh" implies close bodily contact, i.e., that he must not treat her in the manner of the Persians who perform their conjugal duties in their clothes. This provides support for [a ruling of] R. Huna who laid down that a husband who said, "I will not [perform conjugal duties] unless she wears her clothes and I mine" must divorce her and give her also her ketubbah.[19]

The myth that religious Jews are required to make love through a hole in a sheet is nonsense. Pleasure was a concern of the rabbis; they understood that it is enhanced by nudity. In fact, if one of the partners does not wish to have sexual relations in the nude, it is considered grounds for divorce.[20]

A tension exists in rabbinic literature between what the rabbis regard as modest and proper on the one hand and what they know will maximize a couple's pleasure on the other hand. Modesty requires that "scholars of the law not be with their wives too frequently like roosters,"[21] yet even a scholar is responsible for maximizing his wife's pleasure. Rabbinic teachings reflect this tension in their discussions about intercourse by day or night, proper sexual positions, and natural or unnatural sex.

According to tradition, sex should take place at night and in the dark. The Talmud forbids sex during the day or by the light of a lamp.[22] Maimonides teaches that, although intercourse on the

Sabbath is a special mitzvah, if the Sabbath light has not yet gone out and there is no separate room to which they can move, the couple should wait.[23] In fact, midnight was considered the ideal time for intercourse.

Behind this law stands the principle "Love your neighbor as yourself" (Lev. 19:18). The rabbis were concerned that a man might see his wife's blemishes and that she would then become undesirable to him.[24] However, there are exceptions:

> Although intercourse was reserved for the night, if because of one's nature one finds himself forced to sleep at night and ought not be aroused or excited, or if the woman's nature is such that she is overtaken by sleep at night and is not sexually receptive at that time, one is permitted to have intercourse during the day, with due sexual modesty, in order that intercourse be performed with acceptance and love and not by force.[25]

Although they set normative guidelines, the ultimate concern of the talmudic rabbis is maximizing the joy of sex. Traditionally most Jewish couples have made love in the dark out of a sense of modesty, but if a couple finds their sex life enhanced when they make love in the light, they are free to do so.

Similarly, in rabbinic Judaism a tension exists between mandating a particular sexual position for couples and allowing for variety and experimentation. On the one hand, the rabbis recommend the missionary position: "She on top and him below—this is the way of brazenness; she below and him on top—this is the way of proper intercourse."[26] According to Rabbi Johanan ben Dahabai, it is forbidden to "overturn the table" (i.e., practice unnatural intercourse or unusual sexual positions), but the rabbis explicitly disagree with him:

> A man may do whatever he pleases with his wife [at intercourse]. A parable: Meat which comes from the abattoir may be eaten salted, roasted, cooked, or seethed, so with fish from the fishmonger. . . . A woman once came before Rabbi and said, "Rabbi, I set a table before

my husband, but he overturned it." Rabbi replied, "My daughter, the Torah has permitted you to him. What can I do for you?"[27]

Maimonides, usually quite conservative on sexual matters, proves quite liberal on this question:

> A man's wife is permitted to him. Therefore a man may do whatever he wishes with his wife. He may have intercourse with her at any time he wishes and kiss her on whatever limb of her body he wants. He may have natural or unnatural sex, as long as he does not bring forth seed in vain. However, it is a sign of piety not to show too much levity but to sanctify himself at the time of intercourse. . . . A man should not depart from the way of the world and its custom because its ultimate purpose is procreation.[28]

In this passage Maimonides tries to give with the right hand and take away with the left. Although he knows that Jewish law allows experimentation and variety, it nonetheless runs against his own sense of modesty and propriety.

The issue of unnatural sex (*biyah lo ke-darkah*) is particularly difficult from a Jewish perspective. Unnatural sex refers to any sexual activity in which semination does not occur in the traditional place,[29] such as oral sex, anal sex, or what the rabbis termed "threshing within and winnowing without" (premature withdrawal). Talmudic sources talk freely about such sexual activity, permitting it under certain circumstances between husband and wife. Nonetheless there is a concern with the wasteful spilling of seed, which Judaism forbids based on the biblical story of Er and Onan. Tosefot raises this contradiction and cites the position of Rabbi Isaac to resolve it:

> It is not considered like the act of Er and Onan unless it is his intention to destroy the seed and it is his habit to always do so. However, if it is occasional and the desire of his heart is to come upon his wife in an unnatural way, it is permitted.[30]

In other words, unnatural sex is permissible only if it is occasional and not exclusive, and if the intent is mutual pleasure. Both husband and wife must agree on any unnatural forms of sex, for Jewish law forbids a man from forcing his wife into any sexual act against her will.

Not all sexual acts are permissible, however, even within a marriage. For example, the Torah forbids a man to have relations with his wife during her menses and for a specific time period afterward. These laws are euphemistically known as *taharat ha-mishpaḥah* ("family purity"). The next section deals with these laws and their modern relevance in some detail.

Jewish law also forbids sexual intercourse between husband and wife by force, when one of them is drunk, when the husband has decided to divorce his wife, when there is strife, or when the wife fears her husband. Even marital sex must take place between two consenting adults and must be performed out of desire, not fear.[31]

The rabbis of the Talmud disagree on whether a man is permitted to fantasize about another woman when he has sex with his wife:

> ". . . so that you do not follow your heart and eyes in your lustful urge" (Num. 15:39). Deducing from this Rabbi taught: One may not drink out of one goblet and think of another. Rabina said, This is necessary only when both are his wives.[32]

Rabina's opinion permits sexual fantasies about another woman not available in the household. Such fantasies would not threaten a woman's status in her own household as would fantasy about a co-wife. The New Testament prohibition against "lusting in one's heart" is unknown in Judaism. Jewish law is concerned solely with a man's behavior, not with his fantasies. In our own times, some sources in Jewish tradition would permit a man to fantasize about a beautiful but unavailable movie star if it helps intensify lovemaking with his own wife. However, a fantasy that might lead to infidelity (i.e., one about a neighbor's wife) would be inappropriate.

Thus Judaism encourages a high-quality sex life within marriage. A good sex life takes time and effort. If sex becomes an afterthought relegated to a few late nights when both partners are exhausted, the marriage will suffer. On the other hand, if both partners communicate their desires, and if they plan ahead and set aside time for proper sex, the holiness in their marriage can be intensified.

Sex is only a small part of a successful marriage. In my marital counseling, I have seen couples with wonderful sex lives and unhappy marriages and couples with mediocre sex lives and loving, caring marriages. To reach the holiness ideal, a marriage must have joyful sex as well as intimacy, communication, mutual respect, family traditions, a shared vision of building a home together, and, of course, love. Our rabbis taught, "When love is strong, a man and woman can make their bed on a sword's blade. When love grows weak, a bed of sixty cubits is not enough."[33] Marital sex should take place within the context of one of the ultimate rabbinic values—*shalom bayit*, "peace in the household."

THE LAWS OF FAMILY PURITY: A PERSONAL APPROACH[34]

Once a month, after nightfall, my wife keeps a secret appointment. Neither our neighbors, our friends, nor our children know where she goes, although our children sometimes wonder why she returns an hour or so later with her hair wet. Usually my wife drives herself, but sometimes I drive her. When I do, I never park and wait for her; it would be improper for a man to sit in the car outside. I leave and return a half hour later to pick her up.

Once a month, my wife goes to the *mikvah* (ritual bath). In this way she and I observe one of the most ancient and most misunderstood traditions in Judaism. For a week and a half before *mikvah* night we avoid marital relations. As husband and wife we can relate as friends, as partners, and as confidants, but not as lovers. On *mikvah* night we come back together as sexual partners. In doing so we are observing the ancient laws of *mikvah*, known euphemistically as *taharat ha-mishpaḥah* (family purity).

On *mikvah* night my wife carefully showers, washes her hair, removes all makeup, trims her nails, takes off her jewelry, and prepares for the immersion. She prefers to do her preparations at home, although many women prepare right at the *mikvah*. When she immerses herself in the *mikvah*, nothing must come between the water and her body.

The *mikvah* is in a modest building containing a room in which to shower and change and a waiting room with several hair dryers. The ritual bath itself looks like a Jacuzzi at a health club. Regular tap water is piped in, but underneath the bath is a connection to water that has been gathered naturally, from either a spring or a cistern containing rainwater. Naturally gathered water meets the religious requirement that a *mikvah* contain *mayim ḥayim*—"living waters."

To the surprise of many Jews, every major center of Jewish population and many minor centers have a *mikvah*. It is used for conversions of both men and women, by brides before their wedding night, by some Orthodox men before Shabbat and festivals, and by many very Orthodox families to immerse their new dishes. The most important purpose of the *mikvah*, however, is to allow married women to observe the traditional laws of family purity.

On any night a variety of women will be at the *mikvah*. Most are Orthodox; some wear wigs and many keep their heads covered. Some are definitely not Orthodox. Often women come in jeans. The *mikvah* attendant observes each woman as she immerses herself, says the traditional blessing, and then immerses herself twice more. The attendant's job is to ensure that the immersion is total so that even the hair goes under water.

My wife has observed that the *mikvah* attendant plays another role for many of these women. She is like a psychologist with whom they can share family problems and discuss community matters. They know she will never tell, for secrecy, modesty, and discretion are absolute requisites of the job.

To understand the laws of family purity, we need to look at the period of the ancient Temple in Jerusalem. The Torah describes a whole group of laws to be observed in the Temple dealing with the categories of *tahor* and *tamei*. (See Lev. 11–15.) These terms are usually mistranslated as "clean" and "unclean," giving the false impression that they refer to something physical. Actually, *tahor* connotes a state of ritual purity, which permits one to enter the Holy Temple; *tamei* means ritually impure and thus unable to enter the Temple.

According to the Torah, both men and women could become *tahor* or *tamei*. Ritual impurity (*tum'ah*) could result from contact with a dead body, with various animals, by contracting some skin diseases, and from both natural and unnatural flows from the body. A person who became *tamei* was separated from certain holy activities such as Temple worship. One way to become *tahor* once more was to immerse oneself in a *mikvah*. The excavation of a kosher *mikvah* at Massada indicates the antiquity of these laws. After the destruction of the ancient Temple most of the laws of ritual purity were abandoned.

However, one of these laws, *taharat ha-mishpaḥah* (family purity), has remained part of Jewish practice until this day. The Torah teaches: "Do not come near a woman when she is *tamei* with her menstrual flow to uncover her nakedness" (Lev. 18:19). The Torah defines the period of being *tamei* from a menstrual period as seven days (Lev. 15:19). A woman in this state is called a *niddah*. In the second century C.E., Rabbi Meir attempted to give a rationale for this law: "Why did the Torah teach that a woman was in a period of *niddah* for seven days? . . . So that she will be beloved by her husband as on the day she entered the *huppah.*"[35] Absence indeed makes the heart grow fonder. For my wife and I there is some truth to this teaching; *mikvah* night has become a kind of monthly second honeymoon for us.

If a seven-day period of separation were all that the laws of *mikvah* involved, many Jews would probably acknowledge the possible benefits of such a practice. The rabbis of the talmudic period, however, added two religious restrictions which make the laws of family purity difficult for most modern Jews today.

The rabbis' first concern was the possibility of confusion in counting the days of a woman's menstrual period. Another Torah law states, "If a woman has a discharge of blood for many days not at the time of her period . . . when she becomes clean, she shall count seven days" (Lev. 15:25–28). The rabbis, concerned that a woman might confuse such an unnatural flow of blood with her regular menstrual period, ruled that in every case when a woman discharges blood, she must wait a full seven clean days before going to the *mikvah* and resuming marital relations:

> R. Zera stated, The daughters of Israel imposed upon themselves the restriction that even where they observe only a drop of blood the size of a mustard seed, they wait on account of it seven clean days.[36]

This self-imposed stringency nearly doubled the time of separation between husbands and wives.

The rabbis' second concern was that casual contact between husband and wife might lead to sexual intimacy during the forbidden period. They therefore ruled that for the nearly two-week period of ritual impurity husband and wife should neither have physical contact nor sleep in the same bed. Twin beds thus became the norm in traditional Jewish households.

These laws are so strict, so private, and so easy to misunderstand that it is no wonder that the overwhelming majority of Jews have abandoned them. The miracle is that so many Jews have continued to maintain them. Today more communities are building *mikvaot*, many fancier than ever, perhaps reflecting the greater affluence of the Jewish community. Jews seem to be returning to observance.

Why do Jews continue to observe the laws of family purity? For Orthodox Jews, the answer is simple: family purity is part of halakhah, God's law, and is thus binding on all Jews. Many non-Orthodox Jews also observe family purity, sometimes without the rabbinic stringencies mentioned above. Why do they choose to obey these laws?

My wife and I belong to this second group. We have found four reasons for observing the laws of *mikvah*, each of which adds a special dimension to our observance. I call these reasons the philosophical, the symbolic, the feminist, and the traditional.

Philosophical

The laws of family purity make a necessary statement about sexual relations. Our society vacillates between an ascetic and a hedonistic view of sex. The ascetic view associates sex with sin, speaks of the weakness of the flesh, and is embarrassed by sex. The hedonistic view, in reaction, promotes pleasure as the ideal, endorses the *Playboy* philosophy, and condones any activity between consenting adults. Judaism, which rejects both these extremes, teaches that sex is God's gift to humans and is therefore holy.

Note that one who is *tamei* must avoid two holy experiences: entering the Temple and engaging in marital relations. We learn from this that holiness is achieved by separation and self-discipline. The concept of family purity teaches that sexual relations are neither a weakness to be tolerated nor a pleasure to be indulged, but a holy activity, a way of serving God. (See chapter 2 for an expansion on the meaning of holiness in Judaism and the possibility of achieving holiness in sexual relations.)

Symbolic

Rachel Adler beautifully articulated the symbolic meaning of the *mikvah* in an essay in *The First Jewish Catalog* (The Jewish Publication Society, 1973). A woman's monthly period is a nexus point, she explained, between life and death. The flow of blood marks a brush with death; a potential child will not be born. The *mikvah*, in contrast, is a sign of life; its waters are called living waters. Immersion in the *mikvah* signals that the potential begins anew for a baby to be born.

My wife and I felt this symbolism most strongly when we struggled with infertility. Each monthly period became a time of mourning and sadness. Significantly, Judaism outlaws sexual relations during mourning. On the other hand, *mikvah* night became a time of hope: perhaps a child would be born this month. The *mikvah* lady would always say goodbye to my wife with the words, "See you in nine months."[37]

Feminist

For many women, rediscovering the laws of *mikvah* has become part of the Jewish feminist agenda. First, this law is considered one of three classical women's mitzvot. (The other two are lighting Shabbat candles and separating a portion of dough from the *hallah*.)[38] Many women are searching for ways to express their Judaism more actively by wearing *tallesim* or reading from the Torah. The laws of *mikvah* are a classical mitzvah for women directly tied to the cycle of their bodies.

The law also makes an important statement about the relationship between men and women. As a consequence of observing this law, a husband and wife are constrained from treating each other as sexual objects. During part of the month, sex becomes off limits; husband and wife must relate to one another in other ways.

A female Reform rabbi explains one feminist approach to *mikvah:*

> Why then was I, a Reform rabbi and committed feminist, splashing around in the Mikvah? Was I going to make myself "kosher" for my new husband? Hardly. For me, it was an experience of reappropriation. The mikvah has been taken from me as a Jewish woman by sexist interpretations, by my experiences with Orthodox "family purity" committees who run communal mikvaot as Orthodox monopolies, by a history of male biases, fears of menstruation and superstitions. I was going to take back the water.
>
> To take back the water means to see mikvah as a wholly female experience: as Miriam's well gave water to the Israelites so too will the mikvah give strength back to Jewish women. Water is the symbol of birth—now it can be a symbol of rebirth.[39]

Traditional

The most important reason my wife and I observe the laws of *mikvah* is that they are a part of Jewish tradition. Jewish women have kept them alive for four thousand years, and it is spiritually comforting to be part of a long chain of observance. Even if we do not quite understand the reason, we observe these laws because we are Jews who want to maintain the traditions of our people. Many of these traditions are a struggle for us, but I have found that precisely those traditions that cause the greatest struggle can become the most precious to us.

In a suburb of a major Jewish metropolitan area, a group of observant Jews recently wanted to build a *mikvah.* Another group of Jews tried to block them legally, claiming, among other things, that a *mikvah* in the neighborhood would cause traffic jams and other disruptions.

Would that it were true! Nobody expects the great majority of Jews to begin using the *mikvah* once again. Yet a small group of Jewish men and women of all levels of observance are beginning to look seriously at the laws of *mikvah*. Perhaps such a practice can make sex more holy, strengthen marriages, or become a path back to tradition. For these reasons alone, the laws of family purity deserve a second look by all serious Jews.

Perhaps one way to encourage a return to tradition is to relax some of the stringencies. Within normative Judaism as practiced by Orthodox Jews, observing the laws of *niddah* has meant separation for twelve to fourteen days, including the seven clean days. For less traditional couples, observing only the seven biblically prescribed days of separation might make these laws more palatable. Blu Greenberg, an Orthodox rebbetzin who has written some beautiful essays on *mikvah*, has recommended precisely that:

> At certain stages of life, and for certain people, abstention from sex for almost half a month is too difficult to sustain. Perhaps there ought to be a halakhic reconsideration of the biblical time span. At this time of return to ritual and tradition, many more Jewish couples seriously may consider the observance of niddah were it limited to the seven-day period prescribed by biblical law.[40]

Professor David Kraemer, a Conservative authority on rabbinic law, has studied the historical development of the laws of *niddah* and makes a similar recommendation:

> The effect of the laws as currently constituted is this: a man and wife may not enjoy sexual relations for fully one-half of the month, that is, for half of their married life. Alternative sources exhibit a contradictory spirit, however—one which values sexuality and which would likely not tolerate the Niddah law as presently defined.
>
> The Mishnah in Ketubot suggests the proper frequency of sexual relations, taking into account the requirements of different occupations (5:6). According to its provisions, absence of sexual intimacy for fourteen days would be acceptable only for a husband who travels out of town. Otherwise it would be too long. R. Meir says that abstention for a period of this duration will cause a woman, when she rejoins her husband in sexual relations, to be beloved to him as the day of their wedding. The same reason would, I suspect, be untenable

if the period were extended to fourteen days. Finally, in a dispute (Ketubot 5:6) concerning the length of time a husband who has sworn not to have sexual intercourse with his wife may remain married before he must give her a divorce, the School of Shammai describes a 14-day maximum, while the School of Hillel allows for a maximum period of abstention of only seven days (in normal circumstances, approximately the length of her period). The longer duration would, according to Hillel, be offensive to the institution of marriage, and is therefore unacceptable. To express it otherwise, the School of Hillel could not permit the present practice of waiting fourteen days.[41]

In my approach, which sees the sexual laws in Judaism in shades of gray rather than black and white, it is absolutely legitimate for a couple to observe only seven days of separation followed by immersion in a *mikvah*. During the period of separation, sexual intercourse would be avoided but not other forms of touching and intimacy. A couple who wishes to observe the various rabbinic stringencies should certainly be encouraged to do so, but rabbinic fences around the Torah have put the laws of family purity out of reach of most Jewish couples. Through a more liberal approach and proper education, family purity can become another way that couples can achieve holiness within their marriage.

6

SEX WITHOUT BABIES, BABIES WITHOUT SEX

> Our rabbis taught, there are three partners in [the creation of] man. The Holy One, blessed be He, his father and his mother. His father brings forth white seed that produces bones, nerves, nails, the brain in his head, and the white in his eye. His mother brings forth red seed which produces skin, flesh, hair, and the dark of the eye. The Holy One, blessed be He, gives the spirit, the soul, the personality of the face, the sight of the eye, the hearing of the ear, the speech of the mouth, the locomotion of the legs, understanding and wisdom. When the time comes to part from this world, the Holy One, blessed be He, takes His portion, and the part of the mother and father are laid before them.
>
> *Niddah 31a*

THE YOUNG COUPLE came to see me to plan their wedding. They were both well-educated professionals with excellent jobs. I discussed the wedding ceremony, then spoke of the purpose of a Jewish marriage using words like "companionship," "a shared vision," and "building a Jewish home." Then I mentioned the importance of children. The couple stopped me and said, "We have discussed it and decided never to have children. Neither of us wants to sacrifice our careers. Besides, it would be wrong to bring children into the world in its present state."

Another couple came to me for counseling with the opposite problem. They had been infertile for many years, and their doctor wanted to try an experimental procedure that would unite the wife's egg and the husband's sperm in a laboratory. If that was unsuccessful, they were considering using donor eggs. The couple had spoken to another religious leader who had told them, "If God had wanted you to have a baby, you would be pregnant already. What you want to do is wrong."

A third couple that spoke to me after the birth of several children believed their family was complete. The woman was taking the "pill" but was concerned about its long-range effects. She wanted her husband to have a vasectomy, but he refused, citing reasons based on Jewish law.

As a rabbi, I constantly confront counseling situations involving couples who want to have children or to avoid pregnancy, who want to know about using birth control or trying experimental reproductive techniques. What insight can I give each of these couples? Is a marriage in which a couple refuses to have children a legitimate "Jewish marriage"? Should I perform a wedding for such a couple? What does Judaism teach about birth control, vasectomies, and the new reproductive techniques? And how do these questions fit in with the Jewish view of sexuality?

In the animal world, the sexual act is inseparable from procreation. Animals have sex only when they are in heat, just before ovulation; procreation is the usual result. Only human beings have the ability to have sex whenever they choose, independent of procreation.

The separation of the sexual act from procreation, a trait unique to humans, is problematic for many religions. The Catholic Church in particular has taught that every act of sexual intercourse must have the potential for pregnancy; for that reason, all forms of artificial contraception are forbidden. Similarly, the Catholic Church forbids most of the new reproductive techniques, such as in vitro fertilization (inaccurately referred to as "test-tube babies"), as contrary to natural law. In Catholicism there is no compromise in the link between sex and procreation. Protestants have a variety of views on the question, with conservative evangelical Christians holding views close to those of the Catholic Church and liberal Protestants holding views close to those of Judaism.

Judaism teaches that sex has a purpose above and beyond procreation, thus leaving room for a more liberal view of birth control. In addition, there is no Jewish doctrine of natural law; although nature is God's creation, humans have been charged with perfecting it. Judaism consequently holds a more permissive attitude toward the new reproductive techniques. In Judaism it is indeed permissible to have sex without children and children without sex.

Nevertheless, even if God created the sexual act for our pleasure and fulfillment, its vital purpose is still procreation. When God created human beings He said, "Be fertile and increase, fill the earth and master it" (Gen. 1:28). (The first phrase is often translated "Be fruitful and multiply.") In Judaism procreation is not merely a life-style option; it is a commandment.

THE MITZVAH OF PROCREATION[1]

According to tradition, procreation is the first of the 613 commandments which God gave the Jewish people. The holiness ideal in Judaism includes marriage and children. Infertility has long been seen as a tragedy in Jewish tradition; the rabbis considered childlessness a form of death.[2] In contrast, being surrounded by children was considered a great blessing: "Your wife shall be like a fruitful vine within your house; your sons, like olive saplings around your table. So shall the man who fears the Lord be blessed" (Ps. 128:3–4).

The rabbis of the Mishnah laid out the precise requirements of the mitzvah of procreation:

A man should not neglect the commandment of "be fruitful and multiply" unless he already has children. The school of Shammai teaches: two sons. The school of Hillel teaches: a son and a daughter since it says: "male and female He created them." If a man marries a woman and lives with her ten years and they have no children, he cannot neglect it any longer. When he divorces her, she is permitted to marry another. The second husband can wait for her ten more years. If she miscarries, we begin the count from the time of the miscarriage. A man is commanded to be fruitful and multiply, but not a woman. Rabbi Johanan ben Berukah said: Both are commanded as it says, "And God blessed them and said: Be fruitful and multiply."[3]

The most striking feature of this Mishnah is the ending, which features a disagreement between an anonymous teacher (known as *tanna kama*, "the first teacher") and Rabbi Yoḥanan ben Berukah. The former says that women are not obligated to be fruitful and multiply—the accepted halakhah. In traditional Jewish law, procreation is a man's mitzvah: a man must marry and have children whereas a woman is free to remain childless. This ancient interpretation of Jewish law will prove relevant in our study of birth control.

A number of scholars have attempted to explain why women are excluded from the mitzvah of procreation. The Talmud teaches:

Where does this [law] come from? Rabbi Illa said in the name of Rabbi Elazar in the name of Rabbi Shimon: The verse teaches "[Be fruitful and multiply], fill the earth and subdue it." It is the way of a man to subdue the earth, but it is not the way of a woman to subdue it.[4]

In other words, a man is expected to take a more active role by finding a wife and fulfilling the mitzvah. A woman is expected to be more passive; it is inconsistent with feminine modesty for her actively to seek a sexual partner. As the Talmud explains:

The Torah says: "When a man takes a wife" and not "when a woman is taken by a man," because it is the way of a man to search for a wife, and not the way of a woman to search for a husband. It is comparable to a man who loses a possession: who searches for whom? The owner of the possession searches for what he lost. (So a man searches for the rib which he lost.)[5]

This passage demonstrates the rabbinic view that the woman is passive, or at least more subtle, in pursuing sexual relations.[6]

A less sexist, more modern explanation is found in the biblical commentary of Rabbi Meir Simḥa Ha-Kohen of Dvinsk, a scholar of this century:

> It is not amiss to assume that the reason why women are exempt from the obligation of procreation is grounded in the reasonableness of the judgments of the Lord and His ways. The Torah did not impose upon Israel burdens too difficult for a person to bear. . . . Women, whose lives are jeopardized by conception and birth, were not enjoined.[7]

This explanation also has talmudic precedent. The case of Judith, the wife of Rabbi Hiya, who sterilized herself with a cup of roots rather than bear the pain of another childbirth,[8] served as a precedent permitting women to use oral contraceptives.

The Torah states clearly that a man must find a wife and have children. Usually a man becomes responsible for observing the commandments of Judaism when he becomes bar mitzvah, at the age of thirteen. Only one commandment is delayed until the age of eighteen: the requirement of marriage and fatherhood.[9] The Talmud makes twenty the maximum age: "Rava said, and also the school of Rabbi Ishmael taught: Until twenty years God sits and waits for a man to find a wife. When he reaches twenty and hasn't married, God says 'blast his bones.' "[10]

A woman technically is not so obligated. In biblical times, when polygamy was the norm, one wife could be the mother of a man's children and another could be his lover and companion, precisely the situation of Jacob with Leah and Rachel (see Gen. 29, 30) and Elkanah with Peninah and Hannah (see 1 Sam. 1).[11] By the

Middle Ages polygamy was forbidden under Jewish law, and in modern times Jewish law has moved in the direction of equality in marriage (see chapter 3). When a woman marries today, she becomes a partner with her husband in fulfilling the mitzvah of procreation. Having children has become a couple's and not merely a man's mitzvah.

How many children should a couple have? Returning to the Mishnah, the school of Shammai teaches "two sons," derived after the example of Moses, who had two sons. In addition, Shammai believed that the economic and military contributions of sons were of great importance to the Jewish community. For Hillel, the minimum requirement was a son and a daughter, derived from the story of creation, when God created Adam and Eve. For Hillel, to give birth to a son and a daughter was to ensure propagation of the species for a new generation. The Talmud says further that one's children should themselves be capable of having children, ensuring continuation to the next generation. Because some children may not grow to adulthood or may prove infertile, Jewish law requires that a couple not stop with two.

The rabbis quote two prophetic verses as proof that a couple has a continual responsibility to produce children: "He did not create it [the earth] a waste, but formed it for habitation . . ." (Isa. 45:18). People have a duty to continue to produce offspring to inhabit the world. The rabbis also taught that a man who has brought forth children at a young age still has an obligation to do so in his old age. They based this ruling on the verse, "Sow your seed in the morning, and don't hold back your hand in the evening, since you don't know which is going to succeed, the one or the other, or if both are equally good" (Eccles. 11:6). On the basis of this verse, Rabbi Joshua taught, "If a man married a woman in his youth, let him marry in his old age; if he had children in his youth, let him have children in his old age."[12]

Is a man ever relieved from the obligation of procreation? The

Talmud cites the example of Ben Azzai, one of the strongest proponents of marriage and children, who nonetheless remained a bachelor his entire life:

> Ben Azzai said: He who does not engage in propagation of the race
> acts as though he sheds blood and diminishes the divine image in the
> world. . . . They said to Ben Azzai: Some preach well and act well,
> others act well but do not preach well. You, however, preach well
> but do not act well. Ben Azzai replied: But what shall I do, seeing
> that my soul is in love with the Torah; the world can be carried on
> by others.[13]

The rabbis ruled that only in a case such as Ben Azzai's, in which
he is diligently engaged in the study of Torah, can a man forgo the
mitzvah of procreation.

Today many couples have other reasons to remain childless.
Some fear bringing children up in a time of overpopulation or
raising children in a less-than-perfect world. Others cite the real
threat of nuclear catastrophe to justify child-free living. Several
rabbinic sources deal specifically with this issue. A well-known
midrash discusses the response of the Israelites to Pharaoh's decree
that all male children be cast into the river:

> "A certain man of the house of Levi went . . . " (Exod. 2:1). Where
> did he go? R. Judah b. Zebina said that he went to seek counsel of his
> daughter. A Tanna taught: Amram was the greatest man of his genera-
> tion. When he saw that the wicked Pharaoh had decreed: "Every boy
> that is born you shall throw into the Nile" (Exod. 1:22), he said: In
> vain do we labor. He arose and divorced his wife. All the Israelites
> thereupon arose and divorced their wives. His daughter (Miriam) said
> to him: Father, your decree is more severe than Pharaoh's, because
> Pharaoh decreed only against the males whereas you decreed also
> against the females. Pharaoh only decreed concerning this world
> whereas you decreed concerning this world and the world to come.
> In the case of the wicked Pharaoh there is doubt whether his decree
> will be fulfilled or not, whereas in your case, though you are righ-
> teous, it is certain that your decree will be fulfilled, as it is said: "You
> shall decree a thing and it will be established unto you." He (Amram)

arose and took his wife back and they all arose and took their wives back.[14]

A similar passage tells of the prophet Isaiah's visit to King Hezekiah, who was deathly ill. Isaiah says, "Set your affairs in order, for you are going to die; you will not get well" (2 Kings 20:1). The Talmud comments on this story:

> What is the meaning of Isaiah's words "You are going to die; you will not get well"? "You shall die in this world and not live in the world to come." Hezekiah said to him, "Why so bad?" He replied, "Because you did not try to have children." He said, "The reason was because I saw by the holy spirit that the children issuing from me would not be virtuous." He said to him, "What have you to do with the secrets of the Almighty? You should have done what you were commanded, and let the Holy One, blessed be He, do what pleases Him."[15]

The meaning of these passages is clear: let the future bring what it will; the obligation of procreation remains. Having children is a statement of optimism, and Jews are a decidedly optimistic people. The future belongs to the "secrets of God" (Deut. 29:28); our Jewish responsibility is to ensure that our people and our mission are carried on to the next generation.

The mitzvah of procreation takes on a particular urgency after the huge losses the Jewish people suffered in the Holocaust. It will take generations before the Jewish people reaches even the numbers it had before World War II. In America, with a substantial rate of assimilation and an extremely low birth rate, the Jewish people are not even replacing themselves. In response to this sobering reality, rabbis within all movements in Jewish life have called for measures to encourage larger Jewish families. Despite the fact that the world population explosion threatens global resources, the Jews find themselves facing the opposite problem: a worldwide population decline.

God created our sexual organs to give us personal pleasure and self-fulfillment. Nevertheless, He also created them for the greater purpose of populating the world. For Jews, procreation is not merely a life-style option but a serious obligation, an attitude that has affected how Judaism views the use of contraception by both men and women.[16]

BIRTH CONTROL BY THE WIFE: SOURCES

Judaism is relatively permissive with regard to artificial contraception on the part of a woman. First, technically she is not commanded to procreate (although when she marries she joins with her husband in the fulfillment of his mitzvah). Second, her use of birth control does not involve the serious transgression of destroying seed, *hashkhatat zara*. However, religious authorities vary on which purposes and methods of contraception they will permit.

The major talmudic source on which later rulings on birth control are based deals with the use of a *mokh*, an absorbent piece of wool or flax:

> Rabbi Bebai recited before Rabbi Nahman: Three (categories of) women use a mokh: a minor, a pregnant woman, and a nursing woman. A minor lest she become pregnant and die. A pregnant woman because she [otherwise] might cause her foetus to degenerate into a sandal (flat-fish shaped abortion due to superfetation). A nursing woman because [otherwise] she might have to wean her child early and he would die. What age is such a minor? From eleven years and one day to twelve years and one day. One who is under or over this age must carry on her marital intercourse in the usual manner. This is the opinion of R. Meir. The sages however say, The one as well as the other carries on her intercourse in the usual manner and mercy will be vouchsafed from heaven, for it is written in scripture, "The LORD protects the simple." (Ps. 116:6)[17]

This passage deals with therapeutic contraception, that is, contraception to save the life of the mother, a fetus, or a nursing child. Many authorities cite this source when they rule on the broader question of permitting such birth control devices as the diaphragm and the intrauterine device (IUD).

Two opinions on the meaning of this passage are expressed. Rashi (1040–1105) interprets the opinion of Rabbi Meir to mean that the three women *may* use a *mokh*; according to this interpretation the sages say the three women may not. On the other hand, Rabbenu Tam (1100–1171) interprets the opinion of Rabbi Meir to mean that these three women *must* use a *mokh*; in this view the sages say the three women are not required to but may use a *mokh*. Jewish law follows the view of the sages.

Interpreting the sages according to Rashi forces one to take a very strict position on birth control; even three women in danger may not use a *mokh*. Interpreting according to Rabbenu Tam allows a more lenient position; the three women in danger may use a *mokh*, and possibly women not in danger may also use it.

Rashi and Rabbenu Tam also disagree on whether placement of the *mokh* is pre- or postcoital. Rashi says the woman uses it before intercourse. Rabbenu Tam, on the other hand, writes:

> Before intercourse it is certainly forbidden to place a mokh because this is not the natural way of intercourse but rather like spilling one's seed on trees and rocks. Rather if it is placed after intercourse it does not seem like a violation because the man had natural intercourse. . . . The woman places the mokh afterwards because she is not warned about the spilling of seed nor commanded to be fruitful and multiply.[18]

To summarize their views, according to Rashi, Rabbi Meir teaches that the three women may use the *mokh*; the sages teach that the three women may not use a *mokh*, and certainly all other women also may not. The *mokh* is placed before intercourse. According to Rabbenu Tam, Rabbi Meir teaches that the three women must use the *mokh*; the sages teach that the three women may use a *mokh*, and possibly other women also may. The *mokh* is placed after intercourse. Rabbinic authorities have taken either a stringent or a lenient view on birth control depending on whether they have followed Rashi or Rabbenu Tam on each of these questions.

The most lenient view in classical literature is that of Rabbi Solomon Luria. In discussing whether a woman may use a *mokh* if pregnancy presents a danger to her health, he follows Rabbenu Tam on the first question but Rashi on the second:

> Rashi's interpretation seems the correct one in that a precoital mokh is assumed, and it is not improper; it is still normal intercourse, for one body derives its natural gratification from the other. . . . Still the [other] point made by Rabbenu Tam is correct, that even other women may use the mokh and the three women must. . . . The law follows the sages: that the three women need not but they and others may.[19]

According to Luria, as long as normal intercourse can take place and "one body derives natural gratification from the other," birth control is permissible.

The issue of oral contraceptives (the "pill") raises different questions in Jewish law. If a woman is "on the pill," intercourse can take place in a natural way; the issue of spilling seed does not arise. Therefore, an even more permissible approach is possible with oral contraceptives than with the *mokh*.

In discussing the issue of oral contraceptives, the Talmud speaks of a cup of roots taken to prevent pregnancy. Whether the effects of the cup of roots are temporary or permanent is a question that will prove relevant in my discussion of sterilization. The main source on oral contraceptives is the story of Judith, the wife of Rabbi Hiya, mentioned above:

> Judith the wife of R. Hiya, having suffered agonizing pains of childbirth, changed her clothes and appeared before R. Hiya. "Is a woman," she asked, "commanded to propagate the race?" "No," he replied. Relying on this decision, she drank a cup of roots. When her

action finally became known, he exclaimed, "Would that you bore unto me only one more issue of the womb."[20]

Based on this story, the rabbis ruled, "A man is not permitted to drink a cup of roots, but a woman is permitted to drink a cup of roots so that she does not give birth."[21] This precedent seems to allow a permissive ruling on the use of oral contraceptives by a woman.

Extrapolating from the talmudic cases, we can discern a certain rabbinic approach to the issue of birth control. When the mother's health or well-being, or that of a nursing child, is threatened, many religious authorities would permit birth control on the part of the woman. Furthermore, the more natural the method and the less it interferes with the natural pleasure of the sexual act, the more acceptable it is. Because of the last condition, oral contraceptives are the most permissible birth control device.

A question arises whether this permissive approach applies when there is no threat to the mother's health. Many Orthodox authorities have said that it does not. For example, Rabbi Moshe Tendler writes:

> Only the most competent Torah authority, whose piety, erudition and sensitivity to family and social problems are well established, can advise on the complex issue of family planning. In general, only the health requirements of the wife, both physical and psychological, can modify the halakhic disapproval of all contraceptive techniques.[22]

More liberal rabbis have broadened the "psychological requirements" that justify a woman's use of birth control. Based on the biblical verse, "The heart alone knows its bitterness" (Prov. 14:10), they have permitted birth control when pregnancy would threaten the woman's well-being, her marriage, or other children in the family. In their view, only the woman can make that judgment.[23]

Permanent sterilization of a woman through such procedures

as tubal ligation creates a more complex issue. More liberal rabbis, even in the Orthodox camp, have ruled that permanent sterilization is permissible. They base their ruling on the story of Rabbi Hiyya's wife Judith, who, as mentioned earlier, drank a cup of roots that caused permanent sterilization. Tosefot quotes this case and rules, "The laws of sterilization do not apply to women."[24] Many traditional authorities have frowned upon the procedure, however, although no direct biblical or talmudic sources prohibit it. These authorities follow Maimonides, who ruled that although such an act is unpunishable, it is still forbidden (*patur aval asur*).[25]

BIRTH CONTROL BY THE HUSBAND: SOURCES

Judaism is far more restrictive about condoms and other male birth control devices than about women's contraceptive devices. First, unlike a woman, a man is commanded to "be fruitful and multiply." In addition, the use of a condom violates the strict prohibition against the wasting of seed (*hashkhatat zara*).

The classical source in the Torah on the wasting of seed is the story of Judah's sons Er and Onan, and Er's wife Tamar:

> Judah got a wife for Er his first-born; her name was Tamar. But Er, Judah's first-born, was displeasing to the LORD, and the LORD took his life. Then Judah said to Onan: "Join with your brother's wife and do your duty by her as a brother-in-law, and provide offspring for your brother." But Onan, knowing that the seed would not count as his, let it go to waste whenever he joined with his brother's wife, so as not to provide offspring for his brother. What he did was displeasing to the LORD, and He took his life also. (Gen. 38:6–10)

Onan's sin was to spill his seed upon the ground, thus refusing to fulfill his levirate duties. According to the midrash, Er also spilled his seed upon the ground because he did not want to mar Tamar's beauty by making her pregnant.[26] From this story comes the English word "onanism," referring to the wasting of seed.

Numerous rabbinic sources speak on the evils of onanism,

whether through masturbation or through the use of such contraceptive devices as the condom. "Rabbi Elazar said: What is meant
by the verse 'Your hands are full of blood' (Isa. 1:15)? This refers
to those who pollute themselves with their hands."[27] The Zohar
and other mystical literature condemn this act in the harshest
terms. According to the Zohar, onanism is a sin whereby "one
pollutes himself more so than through any other sin in this world
or the next."[28]

In spite of this harsh language, it is difficult to pinpoint the
exact biblical source of the prohibition. The rabbis considered the
story of Onan merely a *remez*, a hint to the law. The story is
complicated by Onan's evil intention of avoiding his levirate duty.
One source has derived the prohibition from the commandment
against adultery,[29] but even this is considered a mere *asmakhta* (a
peg on which to hang a law as a reminder). In other words, *hashkhatat zara* seems to be a rabbinic prohibition with little biblical
support.

The law is not absolute; at times Jewish law permits the spilling
of seed. For example, sexual intercourse is mandated with one's
wife even if there is no chance it will lead to pregnancy because she
is infertile, too old, too young, or already pregnant. In these cases,
no children could possibly result from intercourse. In addition, as
shown, unnatural intercourse is permissible as long as it is occasional and the intention is enjoyment. Also, Jewish tradition permits masturbation for purposes of semen testing or artificial
insemination with the husband's sperm.[30]

A more explicit example is given in the Talmud: "During all
the twenty-four months (of nursing) one may thresh within and
winnow without; these are the words of R. Eliezer. The others said
to him: Such actions are only like the practice of Er and Onan."[31]
Rabbi Eliezer's opinion is not followed in the various codifications
of Jewish law. However, it is fascinating that Rabbi Eliezer, who
usually takes a very strict view, permits coitus interruptus if it

serves a greater good: *onah,* the requirement of regular sexual relations between husband and wife.

Why did the rabbis, without a clear biblical mandate, so strictly condemn the spilling of seed? We can only speculate on the answer. Perhaps it is related to a mistaken understanding of human reproduction.

One modern book on sexuality gives the following explanation:

> At the time of the birth of Jesus, Jews and most other people believed that it was the man and his semen who provided the actual life, the "seed," and that the woman was merely the soil, so to speak, in which the seed grew to maturity to be born. It was considered almost like murder to allow the "seed" to be "wasted" through masturbation, homosexuality, or sexual intercourse without intent to procreate. It was also erroneously believed . . . that semen, "the precious fluid," was limited in quantity so that if it was "wasted" the energy and strength of the man would thereby be reduced.[32]

The severe rabbinic stricture on the wasting of seed is understandable in light of the belief that the male seed was really a person in miniature waiting to be planted in female soil and that the number of such seeds was limited. Nevertheless, as our understanding of the male reproductive system changes, perhaps the law should also change.

Jewish law also prohibits the sterilization of a male, whether by a vasectomy or with drugs, based upon the verse in the Torah: "No one whose testes are crushed or whose member is cut off shall be admitted into the congregation of the LORD" (Deut. 23:2). The Talmud understood this verse to refer to a man who deliberately sterilizes himself as opposed to one who is sterilized in an accident.[33]

These sources clearly indicate that, according to traditional rabbinic law, the male can do nothing either temporarily or permanently that prevents him from fulfilling his God-given mitzvah of procreation. Any contraceptive measures must be taken by the woman.

CONCLUSIONS FOR MODERN JEWS

Based solely on the sources cited here, Jewish law seems to take a rather restrictive view of birth control. Any birth control device used by the husband would be forbidden. According to most authorities, a device used by the wife would be permissible only if it is warranted by health reasons and does not interfere with the natural sexual act. Therefore, the pill is preferable to the diaphragm, and a postcoital spermicide is preferable to any method used before intercourse. Most married couples, with the exception of the very Orthodox, prefer to ignore these laws.

Nevertheless, even liberal Jews can gain insights from studying the traditional sources. Birth control is not a matter of black and white, of permitted or forbidden, within Jewish law. A couple making a decision about contraception should consider the entire Jewish approach to sexuality, marriage, and procreation.

As demonstrated, Judaism regards sex as having purposes above and beyond procreation. When the wife's health or well-being is threatened by pregnancy, she is not expected to be celibate. The Jewish approach prefers sex with contraception to no sex. The tradition sets limits by restricting contraception to the woman and by demanding that the contraception not impede natural intercourse.

More liberal Jews might expand the number of situations in which contraception is justified. For instance, a couple might choose to delay having children in order to have time to strengthen their marriage. They might choose to space their children to give each one the maximum parental attention during their younger years. They may choose to stop having children after reaching the maximum number their emotions and their finances can handle.

Use of contraception in each of these cases can be supported by sources within the tradition.

Nevertheless, Jewish sources cannot be used to justify using birth control to avoid having children altogether. Procreation is not a life-style option but a commandment. Marriage and children are at the center of the Jewish vision of the ideal life, and in light of the Jewish negative population growth, the need for Jewish children is greater than ever.

Modern attempts to liberalize attitudes toward male contraception are more difficult because of the issue of spilling of seed. Even here, however, there is precedent for permitting spilling of seed if the intent is to fulfill a mitzvah and not simply to pour the seed upon the ground. (See Rabbi Eliezer's opinion above.) Furthermore, the notion that the law against spilling seed is based on biological misconceptions may be ample reason for rethinking it.

The Jewish approach to birth control is also concerned that the couple fully enjoy sexual relations by making them as natural as possible. Rabbi Luria, who wrote the most liberal ruling on birth control, uses the phrase *guf ne-enah min ha-guf*—"one body finding enjoyment from another body." In other words, the birth control method a couple chooses ought to enhance mutual enjoyment of the sexual act. Sex can sometimes be most enjoyable when the fear of pregnancy has been removed.

Judaism takes a much stricter stand on sterilization than on birth control, particularly on the issue of vasectomies. Even a liberal Reform rabbi such as Walter Jacob has written:

> While we disagree with tradition on matters of temporary birth control and are more permissive than many of the traditional authorities, we would agree with tradition on this prohibition against permanent sterilization. This is an irreversible act, and should not be undertaken.[34]

Perhaps most important, just as no couple should begin sexual relations without a careful study of birth control options and their effectiveness, so no serious Jewish couple should choose a method of contraception without a careful study of the Jewish issues involved. This includes some soul searching about their motivations for using birth control. Are they seeking contraception to time their pregnancies or to avoid the mitzvah of procreation altogether?

What about the use of contraception by unmarried people? Judaism does not condone nonmarital sex (see chapter 4), so it certainly does not condone birth control devices outside of marriage. Traditional halakhic sources, written for the observant community, do not even raise the issue of birth control by unmarried individuals.

This book takes a different approach, speaking in shades of gray rather than black and white. Although nonmarital sex falls short of the Jewish ideal of holiness, such sexual activity is an undeniable fact of life today, even for otherwise observant couples.

For single people who are sexually active, it is patently irresponsible not to use birth control. In fact, from a Jewish point of view, such usage is more vital for them than for married couples. A married couple may find an accidental pregnancy to be untimely, and it may even create a family crisis, but such a pregnancy does not break with the norms of Jewish marriage.

For a single woman, an unplanned pregnancy raises numerous difficult issues of Jewish law and morality. Abortion as a form of birth control is a serious violation of Jewish law (see chapter 7). Single parenting, although not uncommon, is recognized as less than ideal for imparting Jewish values to children. Rushing into a marriage on account of pregnancy is hardly an auspicious start for a healthy, lifelong relationship. Placing a baby for adoption, an option rarely practiced by Jewish women, is a wrenching emotional decision.[35]

Given these realities, unmarried people who engage in sexual activity, including young people, must have access to birth control information. The same hierarchy of Jewish values would govern their use. A woman's use of contraceptives would be more acceptable than a man's, and the method that caused the least interference with the enjoyment of the sex act is preferred.

These guidelines bring us directly to the issue of condoms. Because they are used by the man and could interfere with the pleasure of sex, condoms are the least permissible method of birth control from a Jewish perspective. Today, however, there is a strong push for condom use as protection not simply against pregnancy but against sexually transmitted diseases, particularly AIDS. For example, a government report on AIDS mailed to every home in the United States writes:

> For those who are sexually active and not limiting their sexual activity to one partner, condoms have been shown to help prevent the spread of sexually transmitted diseases. That is why the use of condoms is recommended to help reduce the spread of AIDS.
>
> Condoms are the best preventive measure against AIDS besides not having sex and practicing safe behavior.[36]

There have been calls for the free distribution of condoms on college campuses and in other places where many individuals are sexually active.

Many Orthodox authorities, such as Rabbi Immanuel Jakobovits, the former Chief Rabbi of Great Britain, have attacked this push for condom use to control the spread of AIDS. To quote Jakobovits, "The condom campaign in effect condones immorality."[37] These Jewish authorities have joined the Catholic Church and other traditional religious leaders in calling for a return to traditional morality, chastity before marriage and fidelity after marriage, as the only totally effective way to prevent the spread of AIDS. They claim that condoms are not only forbidden by Jewish law but are not necessarily always effective.

These religious authorities are correct; condoms are not totally effective, and chastity is still the ideal protection against AIDS. These facts, however, beg the question. The reality is that adults and teens will be sexually active despite the fervent warnings of religious leaders.

If people engage in sexual activity, Jewish law obligates them to take whatever action will be most effective to protect their health. The talmudic dictum states, "It is more stringently forbidden to endanger oneself than simply to break a prohibition."[38] In other words, if people are sexually active, it is better for them to break Jewish law and use condoms than to follow Jewish law and endanger themselves.

THE NEW REPRODUCTIVE TECHNIQUES

As many as 15 percent of married couples are estimated to have infertility problems. The number may be even higher in the Jewish community because so many Jews delay childbirth for educational and professional reasons. Fortunately, new reproductive techniques have allowed many otherwise infertile couples to fulfill their dream of parenthood. These techniques include not only powerful drugs and new surgical techniques but such controversial procedures as in vitro fertilization, artificial insemination with donor sperm, surrogate motherhood, and embryo transplants.

Because these new techniques separate the act of procreation from the act of sexual intercourse, they have been condemned as contrary to natural law and thus declared immoral by the Catholic Church. A recent document issued by the Vatican expresses sympathy with infertile couples but states, "Marriage does not confer upon the spouses the right to have a child, but only the right to perform those natural acts which are per se ordered to procreation."[39]

In contrast, Judaism does not recognize the doctrine of natural law. Nature is God's creation; human beings have been commanded to perfect it. From a Jewish perspective, using new surgical techniques to help an infertile couple have a baby is as permissible as using surgery to help bypass clogged coronary arteries. In fact, one expert has argued that in vitro fertilization should have been termed "fallopian bypass surgery" rather than "test tube babies." Some have claimed that people play God in such medical procedures as in vitro fertilization, yet the same could be said of any medical procedure. I prefer to see our role as that of God's partner; only God can create life, but we can set up conditions that make that creation possible.

Therefore, in principle Judaism does not object when Jewish couples use new reproductive techniques to help them fulfill the mitzvah of procreation. However, each of these techniques raises certain halakhic questions.[40]

The techniques that raise the fewest objections are those in which the father's own sperm and the mother's own egg are used. Most rabbis are permissive on the issue of artificial insemination with the husband's own sperm or in vitro fertilization using the husband's sperm and wife's ovum. In these cases, problems of lineage, so vital to Jewish law, do not arise.

When genetic material is donated, however, the issues become more complex. Many rabbis forbid the donation of sperm, an ovum, or a womb because Jewish law places great emphasis on determining proper lineage. For example, after a divorce a woman must wait three months before remarrying; if she becomes pregnant before the waiting period has elapsed, paternity cannot be clearly established. According to traditional Jewish law, one's status as a Jew is decided by the biological mother. (Other examples are one's status as a Kohen, Levi, or Yisrael, which is decided by the biological father. Similarly, a person is either *kasher* [fit] or a *mamzer* [illegitimate] based on the facts of birth [see chapter 3]. When a child's biological background is unknown, he or she might unwittingly marry a biological sibling. Because of this emphasis on biological lineage, adoption as a formal legal process never developed in Jewish law.[41]

In the case of reproductive techniques, we are therefore faced with a classical dilemma in Jewish law. On the one hand, a primary mitzvah commands us to "be fruitful and multiply." On the other hand, we are similarly commanded to establish proper lineage for a child on both the mother's and the father's side. Can the issue of lineage be overlooked to allow a couple to fulfill the mitzvah of procreation? Which consideration takes precedence?

I contend that the issue of genealogy is secondary to the issue of procreation. Judaism has often been willing to overlook questions of lineage to serve the greater good of the community. For example, as demonstrated, the rabbis were willing to presume non-*mamzer* status even for a child born to a woman twelve months after her husband has gone overseas.

Even biblical precedent exists for ignoring biological facts in establishing legal paternity. According to the law of levirate marriage (Deut. 25:5–10), if a man dies childless, his brother is expected to raise children in the name of the deceased brother. One brother is the sperm donor; the other is the legal father. This case implies that the true father is not the progenitor but the one who gives his name and values to the child.[42] We can draw upon this example as a precedent for permitting artificial insemination with donor sperm.

Some have claimed that artificial insemination by donor constitutes adultery. Jewish law as well as our secular legal system, however, understands adultery as an overt sexual act, not a medical procedure involving the placement of donor sperm in the woman's womb. Based on this principle as well as various talmudic sources, I believe that Judaism can allow a permissive ruling on donor insemination when male infertility has prevented the mitzvah of procreation.

The technique of retrieving donor eggs from a woman and planting the fertilized egg in a different woman, a form of surrogate motherhood, raises similar problems. As mentioned, in Jewish law one's status as a Jew is established by the mother. In this case, who is the mother: the egg donor or the woman who carried the pregnancy to term? Although the issue is still unsettled, a number of Jewish sources seem to indicate that the woman who gives birth establishes a child's identity as a Jew, regardless of the genetic background. Based on this interpretation, if a Jewish woman donates an egg that is transplanted into a gentile woman and the baby is then adopted back by the Jewish woman at birth, the child is considered gentile and would need conversion to become Jewish.

The issue of a donor womb, popularly known as surrogate motherhood, is more complex because of the thorny legal and emotional issues involved. The husband's sperm is used to impregnate a woman other than his wife, who then carries the baby to term. The baby is adopted back by the biological father and his wife, and the woman who carried the baby receives a substantial sum of money for her trouble. Feminists have joined with the Catholic Church and rabbis within all movements in condemning the procedure. The painful Baby M case in New Jersey (1986) has made us conscious of the legal and emotional problems raised by hiring a surrogate mother.

In my own counseling, I have recommended against surrogate motherhood, but not because of religious objections. I have discovered that couples usually pursue this option because they want to maintain a genetic connection with the child. I do not feel such a connection is important enough to justify the legal and emotional risk; I prefer adoption.

Nevertheless, if a husband and wife decide to pursue surrogate motherhood, are able to find a woman to carry their baby, and understand the risks, why shouldn't they be allowed to do so? There are certainly biblical precedents for surrogate motherhood:

Abraham and Sarah used Hagar; Jacob and Rachel used Bilhah. Some have claimed that surrogate motherhood is baby buying, but how can a biological father buy his own child? One can also argue that any money paid to a surrogate mother compensates not for the baby but for the pain and inconvenience of the pregnancy.

Certainly, as in adoption, no birth mother should ever be forced to place her baby against her will. A reasonable waiting period should be established during which the surrogate mother can change her mind. Also, if the birth mother is not Jewish, the baby would have to be converted as in any other adoption.

It is inconsistent for feminists, who have argued for a woman's reproductive rights when it comes to abortion, to forbid a woman the same right to become a surrogate mother. Although some may do so for mercenary reasons, most women become surrogate mothers for altruistic reasons: they have a desire to help an infertile couple. Religious leaders should encourage such women, not condemn them.

Infertile couples who are considering unconventional medical procedures such as those discussed above should have the support and blessing of the religious community. Coping with their own infertility already imposes burdens on them; their suffering should not be exacerbated by community censure. Technology, including reproductive technology, is neither good nor evil but morally neutral.

As with any technology, the new reproductive techniques leave room for abuse. Society must be on guard against such abuse. If properly used, technology can make us partners with God in creation. What greater use can we make of our God-given knowledge than the creation of a new life? What greater gift can we bestow than giving a baby to a couple who would otherwise be childless?

7

JUDAISM: PRO-LIFE AND PRO-CHOICE

> Antoninus said to Rabbi: "From when is the soul endowed in man, from the time of conception or from the time of formation?" Rabbi replied, "From the time of formation." The emperor demurred, "Can meat remain three days without salt and not putrefy? You must concede that the soul enters at conception." Rabbi said, "Antoninus taught me this and scripture supports him as it is said, 'Your providence watched over my spirit'" (Job 10:12).
>
> *Sanhedrin 91b*

I RECENTLY participated in a panel of clergy discussing abortion. To my geographical right and my ideological left sat a Unitarian minister, a mother who passionately advocated the right of a woman to choose abortion. To my geographical left and my ideological right sat a Catholic priest, equally articulate in arguing that abortion is murder. I sat in the middle, charged with the task of presenting a rabbinic perspective.

As the evening went on and we took questions from the audience, the temperature in the room seemed to rise as the discussion grew more heated. Being in the middle, I found myself answering strident questions from both pro-life and pro-choice advocates, many of whom came to the dialogue not to learn but to argue. Over the course of the evening, I noticed that I shared a commonality of language with both my fellow clergy. Although they had difficulty communicating with one another, I could communicate with both of them.

When the evening was over, several people congratulated me on my presentation. What surprised me was that both pro-choice and pro-life advocates were among those congratulating me. It was not that I was so wishy-washy and vague that everyone felt I had agreed with their point of view; on the contrary, I knew that I had presented a clear, passionate argument for the Jewish position. I discovered that night that Judaism has insights that appeal to both sides of the abortion question. By drawing upon the wisdom of rabbinic tradition, we Jews can shed light on today's most divisive and agonizing social issue.

SEARCH FOR A COMMON LANGUAGE

The trouble with the abortion issue is that each side absolutely excludes the other's point of view and is absolutely convinced of the moral rightness of its cause. The sides do not even share a common language in which to debate. What one side calls "fetal tissue," the other side calls "a baby"; what one side calls "a surgical procedure," the other calls "murder"; what one side sees as "a private right," the other sees as "a public responsibility."

Even the terms "pro-life" and "pro-choice" are too emotion-laden to permit reasonable discussion. What does "pro-life" mean? How do antiabortionists who favor capital punishment or military intervention justify their positions? Can someone who is pro-life enjoy hunting? What does "pro-choice" mean? Should society condone all private choices? What about suicide or the use of illegal drugs? Because they are convenient labels, I use "pro-life" and "pro-choice" to describe the pro- and antiabortion rights positions, but I admit from the outset that they are inadequate terms.

In staking out the Jewish position, we must differentiate between the classic rabbinic stance on abortion and the opinions held by many Jews today. Jews do not necessarily draw upon the wells of Jewish tradition in forming their opinions. Some Jews who place themselves staunchly in the pro-life camp are Orthodox, using Orthodox terminology to defend their position. Nevertheless, as I will show, even Orthodox Judaism is vastly more permissive on abortion than either Catholicism or fundamentalist Protestantism. In addition, many non-Orthodox Jews have a powerful conviction that abortion is wrong and that the government should severely restrict its availability.[1]

The majority of Jews place themselves in the opposite camp, advocating freedom of choice and abortion rights. Their position has grown out of a general Jewish identification with liberal and feminist causes as well as a distrust of the Christian fundamentalists who constitute the most vocal antiabortion group. Few Jews who advocate abortion rights have arrived at their conclusion after a careful reading of rabbinic sources and Jewish tradition. I once listened to a liberal rabbi publicly proclaim to a group of Christian clergy that "Judaism condones abortion." A deeper acquaintance with Jewish tradition discloses that it does not, in fact, condone abortion on demand.

Before I describe the Jewish position on abortion, it is useful to choose an emotionally neutral working term for the fetus or unborn child. Our best source is the Hebrew language, which uses various terms depending on the context. A *nafal* (literally "one who fell") is used for the fetus following an abortion or miscarriage and for a baby who dies before it is thirty days old. Although the term will be important in our discussion, it is obviously not useful for a living fetus.

A better term is *ubar*, usually translated "embryo" but referring to both the embryonic and the fetal stages of development. The term appears in numerous contexts in rabbinic literature, some of which have been used to bolster both sides of the abortion issue. For example, Jewish pro-choice advocates have often cited the rabbinic saying *ubar yerakh emo*—"the embryo is a limb of its mother."[2] On the other hand, some usages of the term *ubar* support the pro-life position. For example, the Talmud says, "Even *ubarim* (fetuses) in the womb of their mothers sang the Song of the Sea."[3] The term *ubar*, which provides a common ground that is emotionally neutral to English speakers, is used in the remainder of this chapter.

We are now ready to define the Jewish position. Our first task is to demonstrate how Judaism differs radically from both the pro-life and pro-choice approaches. Only then can we show what Judaism shares with both positions and how it can shed light on the abortion issue.

JUDAISM AND PRO-LIFE: HOW THEY DIFFER

Most (although not all) in the pro-life camp accept the premises that the *ubar* is a human being, that, therefore, to take its life constitutes murder, and that life begins at conception. Although they use various religious or philosophical arguments to bolster their position, pro-life advocates make their strongest case when they state that biologically the *ubar* is no different before birth than after birth. If we are to prohibit murder after birth, we must of necessity outlaw it before birth; if we permit abortion, we must then permit infanticide.

This argument contains an essential fallacy. If the *ubar* is a full human being and abortion is murder, then we ought to punish doctors who perform abortions in the same way that we punish murderers. Are pro-life advocates prepared to sentence physicians to life imprisonment, or possibly even death, for performing abortions? Are pregnant women seeking abortions to be punished? Even the most strident antiabortionists hesitate when confronted with these questions.

In truth, the legal traditions of our society have long differentiated between murder and abortion. The *ubar* may share certain biological qualities with human beings; it may be worthy of our concern and protection as a potential life. From a legal point of view, however, to destroy it does not constitute murder.

Jewish tradition is also unequivocal in stating that *abortion is not murder.* Judaism sees the status of the *ubar* very differently than most people in the pro-life camp see it. According to Jewish law, the *ubar* is not yet fully a human being. To understand this Jewish view, we must first state a postulate that underlies much of Jewish law and theology: one can never put a price on a human life. Jewish tradition separates completely the realm of property matters, *dinei mamonot,* from the realm of human life, *dinei nefashot.*[4] Thus, for example, the Torah explicitly forbids paying a fine (property) as punishment for murder (human life, see Num. 35:31). It insists on "life for life" (Exod. 21:23).

Against the background of this principle, we can understand the central passage in the Torah concerning abortion:

> If men strive together and hurt a woman with child so that her fruit depart, and yet no harm follow, he shall be surely fined. According as the woman's husband shall lay upon him and he shall pay as the judges determine. (Exod. 21:22)

The passage deals not with abortion but with an accidental miscarriage. The Torah mandates a fine, thus situating this case within the realm of property, not murder.

The verse from Exodus is not a blanket permission for abortion, although many rabbis use it that way. It simply states that from a Jewish perspective abortion is not murder. To say abortion is not murder does not automatically imply that it is therefore permissible.

Judaism also differs from the pro-life position on another issue. As a general rule, those who would outlaw abortion focus their attention entirely on the *ubar,* giving little consideration to the other human being involved, the woman. Even in the most

extreme case of therapeutic abortion, the pro-life camp has difficulty justifying the procedure. Why should one life (the *ubar*) be
set aside for another (the mother)? Because of this dilemma, the
Catholic Church has allowed only indirect therapeutic abortion, as
a secondary result of another life-saving procedure.[5]

In contrast, Judaism clearly gives priority to the mother's life
over that of the *ubar*. If her life is threatened, Judaism mandates a
therapeutic abortion. The Mishnah teaches, "If a woman suffer
hard labor in travail, the child must be cut up in her womb and
brought out piecemeal, for her life takes precedence over its life."[6]
Classical commentators disagree, however, on the reasoning behind this law. Rashi argues that abortion is permitted in this case
because the *ubar* is not a full human being *(lav nefesh hu)*.[7] Rambam, on the other hand, permits the therapeutic abortion because
the *ubar* is a pursuer *(rodef)*; thus the procedure becomes an act of
self-defense.[8] Based on this difference, authorities who follow
Rashi tend to be more permissive about abortion than those who
follow Rambam.

Even when her life is not directly threatened, Judaism is concerned with the pain and suffering of the mother. This concern
arises in the Talmud in a rather strange context, the execution of
a pregnant woman. (Note that, although the rabbis discussed capital punishment regarding its theoretical applications, it was rarely
applied in practice.) The Mishnah teaches, "If a (pregnant) woman
is about to be executed, one does not wait for her until she gives
birth."[9] The Talmud remarks that we may even deliberately cause
an abortion to prevent the mother the further shame of a miscarriage during the execution. Delaying the execution until the baby's
birth is considered too painful for the mother. Concern for the
mother's pain has long taken precedence over protection of the
ubar.

Based on this consideration for the mother, many rabbinic
authorities have permitted abortion when carrying the *ubar* to term

would be overwhelmingly painful to the mother or harmful to her well-being. The circumstances under which a particular rabbinic authority would permit abortion vary. They may include threats to the mother's health, pregnancy as a result of rape or incest, and the birth of a seriously deformed baby or one with a dreadful disease such as Tay-Sachs. Rabbinic permission for abortion in these circumstances is handled case by case.

Two examples from the Responsa literature are useful. In the eighteenth century, Rabbi Jacob Emden permitted an abortion following adultery because of the guilt and anguish of the mother.[10] A more recent ruling by Rabbi Yehudah L. Perilman of Minsk permitted an abortion in a case of rape because "she differs from mother earth in that she need not nurture seed implanted within her against her will."[11] In spite of these liberal rulings, no Jewish authority permits abortion because a pregnancy is inconvenient or unwanted.

In summary, Judaism in all its movements including Orthodoxy differs from the general pro-life position in two essential ways. First, abortion is not considered murder. Second, Judaism focuses on the mother's health and well-being; the *ubar* is a lesser concern. Based on these two considerations, many rabbis, particularly those in the liberal camp, have taken a staunch pro-choice position. Nevertheless, Judaism also differs from pro-choice in several ways.

JUDAISM AND PRO-CHOICE: HOW THEY DIFFER

Most pro-choice advocates begin with a presumption which is contrary to rabbinic ethics: that all choices are equally valid and that no moral judgment can be made about any choice. The best example in my experience arose at a talk I once gave on the ethics of abortion. I made what I felt was an innocent comment: "I admire a woman who makes the decision to carry an unwanted

pregnancy to term, despite the easy availability of abortion today."
I was then bitterly attacked by a pro-choice advocate in the audience, who said, "What is there to admire?! She has a choice to do
what she wants, and you have no right to pass judgment one way
or another." I responded that as a rabbi I have a responsibility to
present a Jewish perspective. From a Jewish point of view, not all
choices are equally valid.

The presumption that all choices are equal is based on the
suppositions that abortion is a *non-event* and that the *ubar* is mere
fetal tissue, certainly not a human being. To many pro-choice
advocates it is but a limb of the mother's body. Jewish law, however, uses the statement "the *ubar* is a limb of its mother" only in
very limited contexts. (For example, if a pregnant woman converts,
her *ubar* is also converted.) Nowhere is this principle used to
justify abortion.

The concept of "reproductive rights" implies that a woman
has control over her own body and can remove the unwanted fetal
tissue at will. (In fairness, many who take a public pro-choice
position are personally against abortion but are opposed to any
government regulation of abortion. However, I have found that
those who argue "all choices are equal" constitute a majority of the
pro-choice advocates, and that this argument dominates their rhet-
oric.)

Even if the *ubar* were merely "a limb of its mother's body,"
Jewish ethics would question a woman's right to do what she wants
with it. Judaism sees our bodies as a gift from God and does not
give us sole authority in deciding how to treat them. Jewish law
opposes suicide, the use of drugs, tattoos, and even eating and
drinking to excess. We are not free to do to our bodies what we
please.

Looking at the issue biologically, we must acknowledge that
the *ubar* is not merely a limb of the mother's body like a fingernail
or an appendix. It has a different genetic code. The central philo-

sophical question is whether the *ubar* is merely an aggregate of chemicals or something more. Rav Hisda addresses this question in a key talmudic statement within a passage discussing the rather arcane laws of the priestly offerings: "For the first forty days, the fetus is mere water."[12]

Rav Hisda's statement is the basis for a number of rabbinic rulings that differentiate the *ubar* before and after it is forty days old. If for the first forty days the *ubar* is mere chemicals, after forty days it is regarded as something more than chemicals. Therefore, a miscarriage or abortion that occurs after the *ubar* is forty days old is not considered a non-event. Such an abortion or miscarriage has halakhic consequences. The same laws of ritual impurity apply to the miscarriage as apply to a full-term birth, and one does not perform a *pidyon ha-ben* for a son born subsequently. I often cite these laws to comfort a couple who has suffered a miscarriage to let them know that their loss is not a nonevent. To be consistent, I cannot tell a woman contemplating an abortion after forty days of pregnancy that all choices are morally equivalent.

Significantly, the forty-day cutoff makes sense biologically. Scientists today use neural criteria to determine death, which occurs when there is no longer brain activity. This new definition of death has allowed organ transplants by permitting us to declare a person brain-dead while the heart is kept beating artificially. Even Orthodox rabbis in most cases have accepted the notion of brain death. We can extrapolate from this notion the parallel idea that if life ends when brain activity ceases, it begins when brain activity starts. Scientists have recorded brain waves at about six weeks, matching almost exactly the talmudic criterion of forty days.

Based on these rabbinic considerations, Judaism has outlawed abortion except in certain very limited cases. This prohibition was assumed by rabbinic law, although it is never explicitly stated in the Talmud in regard to Jews. Interestingly, it arises only in a case applying the laws of murder to non-Jews:

On the authority of Rabbi Ishmael it was stated, (a non-Jew is executed) even for the murder of an embryo. What is R. Ishmael's reason? Because the Torah writes: "Whoso sheddeth the blood of man within man, shall his blood be shed" [Gen. 9:6]. What is a man within another man? An embryo in his mother's womb.[13]

This passage was discussed at length by the rabbis both during and after the talmudic period. Is it possible, the rabbis argued, for something to be illegal for non-Jews but legal for Jews? The consensus is that abortion is permitted to both gentiles and Jews only in the limited cases when continued pregnancy would be extremely harmful to the mother.[14] As a general rule, abortion is prohibited both for Jews and Gentiles.

Judaism differs fundamentally from the pro-choice position in that it is unwilling to term abortion a non-event, something which is solely the mother's personal choice. The problem with most pro-choice advocates is that their arguments center totally on the mother (just as pro-life arguments center totally on the *ubar*), ignoring the fact that another entity is involved. According to Jewish law, although the *ubar* may not be a full human being, so that taking its life would not constitute murder, neither is it merely chemicals or a limb of the mother's body, to discard if she desires. To use an analogy in Jewish law, taking the life of a baby before it is thirty days old (considered a *nafal* because vitality has not been proven) does not technically constitute murder. Nevertheless, that fact does not make killing the baby permissible.

One Jewish writer makes this point quite persuasively:

Even though a fetus is not a constitutional person, it is nevertheless an entity of considerable moral and emotional significance in our culture, and a state may recognize and try to protect that significance in ways that fall short of any substantial abridgment of a woman's constitutional right over the use of her own body. A state might properly fear the impact of widespread abortion on its citizens' instinctive respect for the value of human life and their instinctive horror at human destruction or suffering, which are values essential for the maintenance of a just and decent civil society. A political community in which abortion became commonplace and a matter of ethical indifference, like appendectomy, would certainly be a more callous and insensitive community, and it might be a more dangerous one as well.[15]

Judaism breaks with pro-choice advocates on another aspect of this issue. A frequent slogan among pro-choice advocates, "every child a wanted child," posits a false dichotomy between two groups of *ubarim*—wanted and unwanted. To decide whether to carry a pregnancy to term based on a vague criterion such as "wantedness" is foreign to Jewish ethics. Such fuzzy thinking has led to the incongruous situation in which doctors fight to save a premature baby in one ward of a hospital while others abort an *ubar* of exactly the same age and physical development in another. In addition, late-term abortions take place with a medical team standing by in case a baby is born alive, a morally untenable situation.

In truth, many unwanted pregnancies produce desperately wanted and valued babies when carried to term. If a baby is truly unwanted by its biological parents, thousands of childless couples are desperate to adopt and love a baby. Judaism cannot afford to put a label like "unwanted" on any *ubar*. For Jews, life is of ultimate value, regardless of its "wantedness."

Thus Judaism does permit abortion in certain very limited circumstances, but not simply because a pregnancy is unwanted. In this respect, Judaism breaks with those who advocate the right to choose abortion under all conditions.

JUDAISM AND PRO-CHOICE: WHAT THEY SHARE

To restate the Jewish position on abortion that grows out of classical Jewish sources, Judaism attempts to strike a balance between the needs of two entities, the mother and the *ubar*. The mother's life clearly takes priority, and she may seek an abortion in certain cases when her health and well-being are severely threatened. Jewish law may even require an abortion in such a case. However, the existence and needs of the *ubar* are never ignored, even in justifiable cases of abortion. Abortion is not a non-event but does not have the same moral standing as carrying the pregnancy to term.

The difficult question is whether these teachings can be applied to a society like that in the United States, which is struggling with the abortion issue. I believe they can be used to strike a compromise between the pro-life and pro-choice positions.

Who should have the right to decide when an unwanted pregnancy meets the criteria justifying an abortion? Those who would outlaw abortion except when it threatens the mother's life would put the decision into the hands of doctors—the situation in the days before *Roe* v. *Wade*, when a team of physicians on the staff of a hospital served as an ethics committee making decisions about abortion.

Most Jews, no matter what their religious orientation, find it unthinkable to return that kind of power to physicians. The result would be arbitrary decisions regarding abortion, with one hospital or doctor permitting what another would forbid. To prohibit abortions except when granted by medical committees would also mean a return to illegal abortions under possibly dangerous conditions. Most serious from a traditional Jewish perspective would be cases in which Jewish law would permit an abortion but the law of the land would forbid it. Placing such decisions in the hands of doctors would represent a policy of coercion against a religious group. (For example, most rabbis, including several leading Orthodox authorities, permit the abortion of a Tay-Sachs baby, but a law making the mother's health the only criterion would outlaw such an abortion.)

A board of ethicists, composed of clergy, physicians, and psychologists, could be appointed to decide abortions case by case according to the rabbinic criterion "overwhelming pain and suffering to the mother," but it is hard to imagine such a board working fairly. I believe that the woman herself must judge whether abortion is the best solution to a problem pregnancy, for only she knows what constitutes "overwhelming pain and suffering." This view is parallel to a classic Jewish source regarding fasting on Yom Kippur: "R. Jannai said: If the patient says: 'I need food' while the physician says: 'He does not need it,' we hearken to the patient. What is the reason? 'The heart knows its own bitterness' (Prov. 14:10)."[16] A position based on this text agrees with the fundamental pro-choice contention that abortion is a private matter to be decided by a woman in consultation with her physician, her family, and her clergyperson.

In my experience, most Jews, even those who are antiabortion, do not seek government restrictions on a woman's right to choose an abortion. They know too well the abuses that government intrusion might cause. They also regard the movement to outlaw abortions as part of an overall agenda of the fundamentalist Christian right, which advocates numerous positions on other issues inimical to the Jewish community. In this sense, the American Jewish community is pro-choice.

Even acknowledging the pro-choice tendencies of American Jews. I cannot help wondering whether we in America have gone too far in emphasizing a woman's right to an abortion to the exclusion of all other concerns, such as the rights of the *ubar*. The pro-choice camp has become increasingly pro-abortion in recent years, opposing any attempt at reasonable government regulation of the abortion procedure as undermining what they regard as a woman's fundamental right to an abortion. Abortion has become the second most common surgical procedure to circumcision, yet women are not informed about the risks or the alternatives to this option. It is ludicrous that a minor needs parental permission to have her ears pierced but not to have an abortion! Nor does it make sense that the father is legally liable for child support if a baby is carried to term but has no say in the abortion decision. Abortion rights activists have bitterly fought any reasonable attempt by society to recommend a cooling-off period, require counseling, or present a pregnant woman with alternatives.

Some government regulation of abortion seems reasonable. Society certainly has an interest in protecting a woman's right to privacy in making the abortion decision, but as Jewish tradition seems to point out, society has other competing interests, such as ensuring that abortions are not taken lightly. Modern scholars have commented that Rabbi Ishmael's ruling outlawing abortions by non-Jews may have been a protest against the widespread Roman practice of abortion and infanticide.[17] If so, the ruling is equally relevant for our society, which accepts abortion with few moral qualms.

Judaism teaches that the *ubar* is not a full life but is more than mere fetal tissue; it is potential life. The painful questions are: How can the conflicting interests between the mother and the *ubar* be reconciled? Is there room for compromise?

Mary Ann Glendon, a professor of law at Harvard University, has raised and partially answered these questions:

> Perhaps it is fitting that abortion law at present should mirror our wonder as well as our ignorance about the mystery of life, our compassion for women who may be frightened and lonely in the face of a major crisis, and our instinctive uneasiness at terminating a form of innocent human life, whether we call it a fetus, an embryo, a baby, or an unborn child.[18]

Glendon sees the abortion laws in Europe as a valid model for compromise between the pro-life and pro-choice positions. For example, she points out that in France abortion is permitted until the end of the tenth week of pregnancy to any woman "whose condition places her in a situation of distress."[19] The decision is up to the woman herself, a clear pro-choice position. Beyond the tenth week, abortion is permissible only for health reasons or because of fetal disease or deformity.

Even though the ultimate decision rests with the woman, the law attempts to encourage her to carry the pregnancy to term. The physician must furnish her with a brochure stating that abortion is limited by law only to cases of "distress" and explaining the public benefits guaranteed to mothers and children. (Incidentally, these benefits are far more generous in France than in the United States.) The woman and, preferably, her partner must receive counseling, and wait a mandatory period which can be waived only in an emergency.

The gist of Glendon's argument is that law has educational as well as coercive value. The French law imparts twin messages: abortion is permitted early in pregnancy for reasons of distress, and abortion is a last resort that society ought to discourage. The result is clearly a compromise between the pro-life and pro-choice positions. The law in France could not be applied precisely in the United States, but Glendon would like to see similar laws enacted here. She hopes that some kind of consensus about abortion would grow out of the law:

> Law itself often assists in the formation of a consensus, influencing the way people interpret the world around them as well as by communicating that certain values have a privileged place in society. We need only think here of the roles that the equality principle and the enactment of civil rights legislation played in shaping our moral attitudes about racial discrimination.[20]

Although Glendon may not be Jewish, her analysis seems very close to the classical Jewish position on abortion. Jewish tradition recognizes that abortion may sometimes be necessary based on the "pain and suffering of the mother" and that the ultimate choice must lie with the woman herself. Nevertheless, Jewish tradition is not at all pro-abortion. Judaism teaches that, all things being equal, abortion ought to be discouraged. This discouragement can come not only through government restrictions such as those in France but through community education and support of alternatives to abortion. It is here that the Jewish community can link hands with pro-life forces.

JUDAISM AND PRO-LIFE: WHAT THEY SHARE

Judaism regards the artificial termination of the life of the *ubar* as an event that should be undertaken only for the most serious reasons. Thus Jewish tradition discourages abortion performed on the grounds that a pregnancy is unwanted or inconvenient. If a doubt exists as to whether an abortion is justified or not, Jewish law rules against the abortion based on the principle: "When in doubt regarding life or death, we take a lenient (pro-life) position."[21]

Many Jews are appalled at the high rate of abortion today. Without necessarily wanting to outlaw abortion altogether, they would like to see a more positive presentation of alternatives to abortion. Even someone who is pro-choice can admit that today not all choices are presented in a positive light. Choosing to carry an unwanted pregnancy to term and bringing a new life into the world is not publicly encouraged, particularly within the Jewish community; yet we are a community deeply concerned with our negative population growth.

The time has come to establish a support network, perhaps called the Jewish Abortion Alternative, with the purpose of providing education on the classical Jewish outlook on abortion. It would also support young women who wish to carry unwanted pregnancies to term with counseling, schooling, housing, medical care, and, if necessary, adoption services. A pro-life choice can be presented as an authentic Jewish alternative, one a Jewish woman can choose knowing that she has the support of the Jewish community.

The Jewish Abortion Alternative could also sponsor a hot line offering twenty-four-hour-a-day counseling for a woman in need. It is a shame that only Christian fundamentalists and the Catholic Church currently offer such services. Counseling would be nonjudgmental—after all, sometimes abortion is the preferable Jewish alternative—but not totally value free; it would reflect the Jewish perspective that abortion is not desirable except in the most extreme situations.

If a woman chooses to carry a pregnancy to term, a full support system should be available to her. A woman in this situation often needs a place to live, maternity clothes, medical care, a supportive counselor, and possibly even a labor coach to be with her during the birth process. It should be possible to establish a network of homes around the country prepared to house such a woman, along with a network of physicians, counselors, and other supportive personnel to work with her.

I would like to see adoption presented to a young woman as a more positive option. A fundamental contradiction now exists in the adoption scene. If a couple adopts a baby, everyone says, "How wonderful!" but if a woman places a baby for adoption, the usual reaction is, "How can she give up her own baby?" No woman should ever be pressured to place a baby for adoption; on the other hand, the choice to make an adoption plan can be presented more positively than it has until now.

If a woman chooses to keep her baby, she needs ongoing support after birth, including financial help and information about available community services. Synagogues can provide membership for a woman in such circumstances as well as a religious education for her child. Certainly, a Jewish community concerned with low fertility rates ought to do whatever it can to help a woman who chooses to bring another Jew into the world.

I realize that most of my recommendations sound foreign to Jewish ears. We are not used to our daughters becoming pregnant out of wedlock. When they do, the easiest option is to arrange a quick and secretive abortion. I wonder, however, whether so many Jews turn to abortion because no humane and supportive alternative is available within the Jewish community.

I hope that the Jewish community in the United States can establish an organization like the one described above. Such an organization, called "Just One Life" *(Nefesh Ahat b'Yisrael),* already exists in Israel.[22] There it is nonpolitical, seeking to educate women and support them rather than to change the law. Such an organization here could serve our classical role as "a light among the nations" (Isa. 49:6) and would appeal to the vast majority of reasonable Americans. Opinion polls have shown that most Americans follow the Jewish approach of being pro-choice and opposed to government prohibition of abortion. At the same time, most are also pro-life in that they are uncomfortable with the procedure itself. The Jewish approach has shown that one can be pro-choice without necessarily being pro-abortion and that one ought to consider all choices, including the choice of carrying a pregnancy to term. The Jewish Abortion Alternative would represent an authentic Jewish approach that is both pro-choice and pro-life.

8

GAY AND JEWISH

"You shall not copy the practices of the land of
Egypt where you dwelt, or of the land of Canaan to
which I am taking you" (Lev. 18:3). What did they
do? A man would marry a man and a woman would
marry a woman.

Sifra 9:8

RECENTLY I was called upon to testify before my local city
council on a proposed gay rights bill. The bill had generated much
controversy in the religious community, with clergy, including
rabbis, lined up on both sides. Before deciding whether or not to
testify, I asked myself, Is homosexuality a perversion that runs
against the family values our society should encourage? Or are gays
a minority group, victimized by hatred and discrimination and
worthy of legal protection? After careful consideration, I chose to
speak out in favor of the bill.

Homosexuality creates a dilemma for rabbis and other Jewish
leaders. On the one hand, the Torah clearly condemns sexual
activity between two men. (Interestingly, it is silent about lesbianism.) On the other hand, there are Jewish gays. Every major metropolitan area in the United States has a gay and lesbian synagogue;
these synagogues have sought recognition by federations and other
communal organizations. Israel also has a number of gay synagogues. Gays have come out of the closet and are active in political
and communal affairs; they have published articles and books on
being gay and Jewish. A number of gay rabbis have publicly revealed their sexual orientation. There is even an organization called

the World Congress of Gay and Lesbian Jews (P.O. Box 18961, Washington, D.C. 20036), and international conferences have been held for gay Jews.

The relationship between Judaism and homosexuality raises a number of difficult questions: How should the organized Jewish community react to Jews who are gay? Is there a link between antisemitism and homophobia? Why have societies with the least tolerance toward Jews also displayed the most hatred toward gays? Like Jews, gays were victims of Nazi Germany. What do the two groups have in common? Should their shared fate not force the Jewish community to confront its own attitude toward gays in its quest to build a more tolerant, compassionate society?

The AIDS (acquired immunodeficiency syndrome) epidemic which has taken the lives of thousands of gay men, many of them Jewish, has also raised questions. How do we give compassionate care to someone with a fatal disease that many consider a punishment from God? When a gay man dies, can his life partner participate in the Jewish mourning rituals? Do we change our treatment of an illness when the sufferer's life-style was a contributing cause? How can the Jewish community help persons with AIDS? Certainly, AIDS has legitimized homophobia and gay bashing, often called the one socially acceptable form of bigotry, but it has also energized the gay community in its search for a cure.

These broad, difficult questions call for answers, but my own interaction with the gay community has been much more personal. Numerous gay Jews who have come to me for counseling have wanted answers that both were authentically Jewish and respected their integrity as sexual human beings.

One man who spoke to me after breaking up with his gay lover was an observant Jew who attended synagogue every Sabbath and festival and strictly observed the dietary laws. He wanted someone whom he could love and who would respect his religious observance. He told me, "I used to go to bars and bathhouses. There was so much promiscuity! It was ugly, wild, not the Jewish way of living." He was looking for fidelity and commitment, which he considered Jewish values. What guidance could I give this man?

Similarly, a married woman who had a young daughter came to me for counseling because she was sexually unhappy with her husband. After several counseling sessions, she revealed that she had lesbian leanings, was sexually attracted to a woman friend, and was debating whether to sacrifice her marriage to find sexual fulfillment in a relationship with a woman. She felt forced to choose between her family and her happiness. How could I help her?

Dealing with parents of gays is especially difficult. Most of us have dreams for our children, which include marriage and family. We ourselves want grandchildren. A child's announcement that he or she is gay strikes at the very heart of a parent's dream. The parents of gays with whom I have met are confused and hurt, confronting a life-style they often do not understand. They feel badly for their child, who will almost certainly face discrimination and bigotry, and they fear AIDS. (Sometimes they first find out that their child is gay when he contracts AIDS.) Often they feel guilty, asking themselves what they did to make their child gay. In most cases the parents must give up their dream of escorting their child to the marriage canopy and seeing the birth of grandchildren.

I have confronted the situations described above a number of times in my rabbinic career and have never found them easy to handle. In the introduction I wrote that a rabbi must walk the line between Aaron and Moses, between loving Jews and loving Judaism. In no area is such a mandate more difficult than in dealing with Jews who are gay. To begin our search for an answer, let us look at the traditional approach to homosexuality as it developed in Jewish sources.

HALAKHAH AND HOMOSEXUALITY

An important point to make from the outset is that Jewish law does *not* teach that it is forbidden to be a homosexual. On the contrary, Jewish law is concerned not with the source of a person's erotic urges nor with inner feelings, but with acts. The Torah forbids the homosexual *act*, known as *mishkav zakhar*, but has nothing to say about homosexuality as a state of being or a personal inclination.

One Orthodox rabbi makes this point explicitly:

> Judaism unequivocally proscribes homosexual practices, but does not blame individuals for being afflicted with pathological homosexual preferences. What is frowned upon by the halakhah is the indulgence in homosexual acts—not the experience of sexual preferences. On the contrary, individuals with homosexual preferences are encouraged by the halakhah to practice self-control and to restrain whatever urges cannot be legitimately satisfied.[1]

In other words, a person with a homosexual inclination can be an entirely observant Jew as long as he or she does not act out that inclination.

The basis of the prohibition against homosexual acts derives from two biblical verses in Leviticus: "Do not lie with a male as one lies with a woman; it is an abhorrence" (Lev. 18:22) and "If a man lies with a male as one lies with a woman, the two of them have done an abhorrent thing; they shall be put to death—their bloodguilt is upon them" (Lev. 20:13). The Torah considers a homosexual act between two men to be an abhorrent thing (*to'evah*), punishable by death—a strong prohibition.

The Torah gives no reason for this commandment. Some commentators have looked for a rationale in the story of Sodom, in which the men in the town attempt to rape the visitors to Lot's house. (See Gen. 19; the word "sodomy" comes from this incident.) However, the occurrence in the story was a case of homosexual rape, hardly a legitimate precedent for the kind of consensual homosexual acts we are considering. Others see the root of the prohibition in the verse "No Israelite woman shall be a cult prostitute, nor shall any Israelite man be a cult prostitute" (Deut. 23:18). Cultic prostitution, both hetero- and homosexual, was a common feature of idolatrous worship in the ancient Near East, but, like the story of Sodom, it is no longer a relevant precedent for modern homosexuality.

Various rabbis have tried to come up with other reasons for the biblical prohibition of *mishkav zakhar*. (Note, however, that a Torah prohibition always stands on its own even if no cogent rationale can be found for it.) Some rabbis have argued that homosexuality is forbidden because procreation is impossible.[2] Others have defined the homosexual act as intrinsically unnatural and therefore opposed to the purposes of creation.[3] There are difficulties, however, with both explanations. Judaism grants sexuality a purpose above and beyond procreation, and natural law, although influential in the Catholic Church, is not an authentic Jewish concept.

A more likely explanation for the ban against homosexual behavior is given in the Talmud by Bar Kapparah, who makes a play on the word *to'evah* ("abomination"), claiming that it means *to'eh atah ba* ("you go astray because of it").[4] Both Tosefot and the Asheri comment on this passage that a man will leave his wife and family to pursue a relationship with another man. In other words, homosexuality undermines and threatens the Jewish ideal of family life, of marriage and children, articulated in the Torah. Heterosexuality is the communal norm for Jews; homosexuality, a perversion of that norm.

Another modern Orthodox thinker makes the point clearly:

> At the outset, it should be stated that when Judaism prescribes norms, these are norms for the entire community, and they are geared towards enhancing that community. Any individual may claim that

he is the exception, and that his own deviance will not harm the community; but the Judaic view has always been that either everyone adheres to the norms, or no one adheres.[5]

Rabbinic literature assumes that Jews are not homosexual. For example, the Mishnah presents the following disagreement between Rabbi Judah and the Sages: "R. Judah said: A bachelor should not herd animals, nor should two bachelors share a single blanket. The Sages permit it."[6] The halakhah follows the Sages because the Talmud says, "Israel is not suspected of homosexuality."[7]

The *Shulḥan Arukh* never explicitly mentions the prohibition against homosexual acts but mentions the precaution that a male should not be alone with another male because of lewdness "in our times." However, Rabbi Joel Sirkes ruled about one hundred years later that such precautions were unnecessary because of the rarity of such acts among Polish Jewry.[8]

A more recent responsum was brought by Rabbi Abraham Isaac Kook, chief rabbi in Palestine. A rumor that a certain *shoḥet* (ritual slaughterer) had committed a homosexual act provoked the question whether he should be disqualified for the position. Rav Kook ruled that the *shoḥet* could be retained because, even if the rumor were true, the man might have since repented of his act.[9] It is noteworthy that Rabbi Kook's responsum considers homosexuality an act of volition for which one can repent.

Lesbianism is never mentioned in the Torah. One talmudic passage refers to homosexual acts between women: "R. Huna taught, Women who have sex one with the other are forbidden to marry a Kohen."[10] The halakhah rejects Rav Huna's opinion and allows a lesbian to marry a Kohen. However, Maimonides ruled that lesbianism is still prohibited and should be punished by flagellation.[11] The prohibition is not as stringent as that against male homosexuality because the Torah does not explicitly prohibit lesbianism and because lesbianism does not involve the spilling of seed.

We can now summarize the classical halakhic position:

1. Judaism is concerned with explicit acts, not inner feelings.
2. A homosexual act between two men is explicitly forbidden in the Torah.
3. A homosexual act between two women is forbidden by the rabbis.
4. Homosexuality is considered an act of volition for which one can repent.
5. The reason for the prohibitions seems to be that such behavior undermines the Jewish family ideal of marriage and children as set out in the Torah.
6. Rabbinic thinkers in the past did not consider homosexuality a Jewish behavior problem.

MODERN RABBINIC RESPONSES

A number of modern rabbis from various movements have attempted to interpret the traditional sources on homosexuality as they apply to gay Jews today. Three basic approaches seem to emerge: (1) a reaffirmation of the traditional prohibition, tempered by a call for compassion for homosexuals (i.e., reject the sin, not the sinner); (2) a rejection of the traditional prohibition in favor of fully embracing the sexual needs of gays; and (3) an attempt to rework the halakhah in light of our modern scientific understanding of homosexuality.

One of the most articulate spokesmen for the first approach is Rabbi Norman Lamm, president of the Orthodox Yeshiva University. He contrasts four different attitudes toward homosexuality: repressive, practical, permissive, and psychological. The repressive approach calls for no leniency but rather social ostracism and possibly imprisonment to protect the moral fiber of society. The practical approach is neutral, avoiding any judgment of homosexuality. The permissive approach views homosexuality as a legitimate life-style. The psychological approach sees homosexuality as a pathology which can be treated as an illness, thereby removing moral culpability.

Lamm definitely prefers the last approach. He writes:

> Homosexuality is no different from any other anti-social or anti-halakhic act, where it is legitimate to distinguish between the objective act itself, including its social and moral consequences, and the mentality and inner development of the person who perpetuates the act. For example, if a man murders in a cold and calculating fashion for reasons of profit, the act is criminal and the transgressor is criminal. If, however, a psychotic murders, the transgressor is diseased rather than criminal, but the objective act itself remains a criminal one. . . . To use halakhic terminology, the objective crime remains a ma'aseh averah (forbidden act) whereas the person who transgresses is considered innocent on the grounds of "ones" (force beyond one's control).[12]

Using the psychological approach, Lamm recommends compassion for those suffering from the homosexual "illness" while condemning the homosexual act itself.

Conservative Rabbi David Feldman takes a similar approach:

> Much of the Jewish sexual code, moreover, has as its purpose—to the extent that we can speak of the law's purpose—the preservation of the marriage bond and the family unit. In an age of family dissolution it is all the more urgent to assert the stance of halakhah against an antithetical life-style.
>
>   . . . moral lapses are not made respectable. However, while sincere, even non-patronizing, empathy may be called for, condonation of homosexuality as an alternate way of life is not.[13]

Feldman teaches that there is no room in Jewish morality to condone homosexuality even if we show compassion for individual homosexuals.

The second approach rejects the halakhah in order to embrace homosexuality fully as a legitimate expression of the sexual needs of many Jews. Advocates of this approach point to the fact that homosexuals have no choice because sexual preference is established at a young age by heredity, environmental factors, or both. An articulate spokesman for this point of view is the late Rabbi Hershel Matt of the Conservative movement:

> The crucial question, however, is whether homosexuality in contemporary society is to be identified with what the Torah forbade—whether, that is, the ancient and modern significance and consequences of homosexuality are the same and whether homosexuality today is inherently idolatrous, immoral, and destructive of Jewish existence. The answer to the question involves, once again, the issue of free choice: are homosexuals able to choose and to change? If they are, they should be considered in violation of the Torah's prohibition, which is still binding; if they are not, but except for the sexual identity of their mate do live faithfully by traditional Jewish standards, they should be fully accepted and respected.[14]

Rabbi Matt continues:

> Those of us . . . who insist that it is God's "right" to prescribe standards for human behavior in general and for Jewish behavior in particular, and who teach that heterosexual behavior is God's intended norm, must not be so presumptuous as to deny God's "right" to create or permit the "homosexual exceptions." Indeed, with regard to such "exceptions" we must strive to echo and to mediate God's full acceptance and approval.[15]

According to Matt, modern homosexuals, who have no choice in their orientation, ought to be exceptions to the traditional halakhah. The trouble with his approach is that halakhah does not work that way. As a legal system, it is binding upon all Jews; to define a list of exceptions is to undermine the halakhic system. For this reason many Jewish gay rights advocates prefer to reject the halakhah altogether.

Rabbi Janet Marder of the Reform movement, who served as

rabbi of the gay synagogue Beth Chayim Chadashim in Los Angeles, takes this radical approach:

> I believe, and I teach my congregants, that Jewish law condemns their way of life. But I teach also that I cannot accept that law as authoritative. It belongs to me, it is part of my history, but it has no binding claim on me. In my view, the Jewish condemnation of homosexuality is the work of human beings—limited, imperfect, fearful of what is different and, above all, concerned with ensuring tribal survival. In short, I think our ancestors were wrong about a number of things, and homosexuality is one of them.
>
> . . . In fact, the Jewish values and principles which I regard as eternal, transcendent and divinely ordained do not condemn homosexuality. The Judaism I cherish and affirm teaches love of humanity, respect for the spark of divinity in every person and the human right to live with dignity. The God I worship endorses loving, responsible and committed human relationships, regardless of the sex of the persons involved.[16]

Rabbi Marder embraces gays by rejecting the halakhah.

Some commentators have gone even farther by saying that an authentic Jewish theology must reject any repression of the inner sexual drive. True spirituality, they claim, can be found only in relationships, which must grow out of authentic erotic urges. For gays to deny their sexuality is to remove themselves from God; to avoid relationships because the Bible forbids them is to live a life of incompleteness. The most articulate spokesman for this approach is Christian theologian James B. Nelson:

> God . . . is the "Cosmic Lover," ceaselessly and unfailingly in action as love. God's abiding purpose for humankind is that in response to divine action we should realize our intended humanity as human lovers—in the richest, broadest, and most responsible sense of the term.
>
> . . . As persons our sexuality means the possibility of expressing and sharing a total personal relationship in love, a relationship which contributes immeasurably toward our intended destiny. . . . Gay

persons desire and need deep and lasting relationships just as do heterosexuals, and appropriate genital expression should be denied to neither.[17]

One Jewish thinker who has developed Nelson's ideas in a Jewish context is Judith Plaskow, who calls for a new theology of sexuality connected to spirituality:

> If we see sexuality as part of what enables us to reach out beyond ourselves, and thus as a fundamental ingredient in our spirituality, then the issue of homosexuality must be placed in a somewhat differ-ent framework from those in which it is most often discussed. The question of the morality of homosexuality becomes one not of hala-khah or the right to privacy or freedom of choice, but the affirmation of the value to the individual and society of each of us being able to find that place within ourselves where sexuality and spirituality come together. It is possible that some or many of us for whom the connec-tions between sexuality and deeper sources of personal and spiritual power emerge most richly, or only, with those of the same sex could choose to lead heterosexual lives for the sake of conformity to hala-khah or wider social pressures and values. But this choice would then violate the deeper vision offered by the Jewish tradition that sexuality can be a medium for the experience and reunification of God.[18]

Plaskow maintains that for a homosexual to be involved in a heterosexual relationship out of conformity to halakhic standards would be a transgression. A gay man or woman can find true spirituality, which is the ultimate goal of the Torah, only in a living homosexual relationship. To Plaskow, not only is homosexuality not a sin, it becomes a mitzvah.

A third approach neither affirms nor denies the traditional halakhic rejection of the homosexual act. Rabbi Robert Kirschner has pointed out that almost everybody, both liberals and tradition-alists, who has written on the homosexuality question has argued that halakhah and homosexuality are irreconcilable.[19] This conclu-sion is based on the notion that halakhah is monolithic and unchangeable. Kirschner argues that halakhah can change and, indeed, has changed when new scientific knowledge has emerged.

Kirschner uses the example of the *heresh*, or deaf-mute, who by talmudic law was considered lacking in mental capacity. As our understanding of deafness and our ability to teach the hearing-impaired to communicate has changed, so has the halakhic status of the *heresh*. Today almost all rabbis consider a *heresh* to have full legal capacity.

Similarly, as our understanding of gays has changed, the halakhah must incorporate that new understanding. Kirschner writes, "Ancient and medieval halakhic authorities assume that homosexuality is a matter of volition. A person engages in it willfully and with wrongful intent. Homosexuality is punishable because it is defined as intentional."[20] Through a survey of modern scientific literature, he shows that homosexuality is a matter not of inner volition but of various genetic and environmental factors beyond one's control. He concludes that, from a scientific viewpoint, "homosexuality appears to be an expression of diversity rather than of perversity."[21]

Kirschner does not examine the full halakhic consequences of the change in how homosexuality is empirically understood. He calls for greater compassion and a recognition that "all persons, in their unique sexual being, are the work of God's hands and the bearers of God's image,"[22] but he does not provide guidelines for resolving such practical questions as gay marriages, gay synagogues, gay rabbis, or the adoption of children by gay couples. He avoids these difficult questions by concluding that the issue *tzarikh iyyun* (needs further investigation).

None of these approaches is totally satisfactory to rabbis like myself, who feel bound by the halakhic tradition yet understand the profound dilemma faced by gay Jews who want to live Jewish lives. The entire question calls for a more pragmatic solution.

A PRAGMATIC CONCLUSION

Finding a halakhically authentic answer to the question of gay Jews is difficult. The Torah unequivocally sets out a strict vision of Jewish family life, which includes marriage and children. In truth, Jewish tradition has little tolerance for deviance. Jews who do not fit into its norms often feel that they do not belong, whether they are single, intermarried, divorced, childless, handicapped—or gay.

The halakhah does not regard all life choices as equally authentic. The Jewish preference is for heterosexual marriage and children. In its recent decision to ordain homosexual rabbis, the Reform Movement clearly reaffirmed this perspective: "In the Jewish tradition, heterosexual, monogamous, procreative marriage is the ideal human relationship."[23] What about Jews who, for reasons beyond their own control, are unable to participate in a satisfying heterosexual relationship? Can we reach out to gay Jews, treat them with compassion, and involve them in Jewish life without compromising the halakhic ideal of marriage and family? That to me is the essence of the problem.

I ask the same question of other Jews who, for many reasons, do not fit the norm: How can I as a rabbi reach out to intermarried Jews while maintaining the stricture against intermarriage? How can I comfort infertile Jews while maintaining the centrality of the mitzvah of procreation? How can I counsel Jews seeking a divorce while teaching that divorce ought to be a sad last resort for a troubled marriage? Once again, I am walking the tightrope between what Judaism teaches and how today's Jews live.

The solution is to view Judaism not in terms of black and white but in shades of gray—to resort to the ladder of holiness described in chapter 2. The holiness ideal in Judaism is marriage and family. Some Jews, for a variety of reasons, cannot live by that ideal. Experts say gays have no choice regarding their sexual preference. These Jews are not sinners but are simply in a different place on the ladder of holiness; they must seek holiness in a different context.

To see halakhah in black-or-white, permitted-or-forbidden terms is to give a gay Jew a choice of either heterosexual marriage or a life of celibacy. A heterosexual marriage for a gay Jew would lead to a life of sexual frustration, unhappiness, and incompleteness, and it would be unfair for the spouse to be trapped in a marriage without hope of sexual fulfillment. On the other hand, a life of celibacy is a tragedy in Jewish tradition. God created humans as sexual creatures; to deny one's sexuality for a lifetime is to frustrate God's design.

If we interpret Jewish tradition in shades of gray, however, alternatives emerge. Holiness is possible even within a gay relationship, one that embraces other Jewish values discussed in this book: love and respect for one's sexual partner, fidelity and trust, concern for sexual fulfillment, and, of course, modesty.

Understandably, too often the values of love, fidelity, and modesty have been missing from the gay community. In a drive to fight sexual repression and low self-esteem, many gays have embraced an ethic of promiscuity and public displays of sexuality. The worst manifestation of this trend is the practice known as "outing," the attempt by many gays to force other gays out of the closet by public disclosure of their sexual orientation.

Judaism teaches that holiness is achieved through privacy, discretion, and modesty. A person's sexual life should never be open for public disclosure. Someone living in an exclusive sexual relationship with another person has no reason to disclose details to anybody except a physician, therapist, or member of the clergy.

The search for Jewish values within gay relationships has characterized the writings of many gay Jews. A recent anthology of essays, *Twice Blessed*,[24] clearly reflects this approach. One review of the book states:

Essayist after essayist insists, sometimes in a plaintive tone that attests to the argument's fragility, that their relationships, too, are marked by emotional intimacy and stability, mutual faithfulness, and economic interdependence; that, like good Jews everywhere, they resist sexual expression outside the confines of the committed couple, dutifully suppressing any impulse toward erotic adventuring, vigilantly exercising sexual restraint.[25]

A pragmatic approach reaffirms the view of the essayists in *Twice Blessed* on the importance of fidelity, modesty, and holiness in gay relationships.

The pragmatic approach suggests a number of practical consequences for the Jewish community. First, Jews must take a strong, public stand in favor of nondiscrimination based on sexual orientation. The human rights to live and to work where one chooses, regardless of color, nationality, sex, or sexual preference, are fundamental, based on the principle that all human beings are created in God's image and deserve to be treated with dignity and to live without fear.

Jews ought to work to repeal all sodomy statutes. Private sexual behavior between consenting adults is not and ought not to be the concern of government. The statutes are not only wrong; they are unenforceable unless the government uses such immoral procedures as entrapment. The call to repeal all sodomy statutes runs directly counter to Rabbi Norman Lamm's recommendation:

The laws must remain on the books, but by mutual consent of judiciary and police, be unenforced. This approximates to what lawyers call "the chilling effect," and is the nearest one can come to the category so well known in the halakhah, whereby strong disapproval is expressed by affirming a halakhic prohibition, yet no punishment is mandated.[26]

Lamm's approach serves only to foster a disrespect for the law as well as to give ammunition to those who continue to discriminate against gays.

The question of gays within the Jewish community is more difficult. How should Jews respond to gay synagogues, the ordination of gay rabbis and cantors, and the solemnization of gay marriages? How can rabbis help gay Jews and their parents in counseling situations?

First, in an ideal world, every synagogue would be open to every Jew. Gay Jews ought to feel at home in any synagogue and not feel the need to form separate synagogues of their own. Unfortunately, we do not live in that ideal world, so we can understand the need for synagogues that reach out especially to the gay community. Because such synagogues can be a vehicle for Jewish observance, Jewish learning, and holiness in the gay community, Jews ought to look with favor at them. Such synagogues should share in the larger Jewish community; federations and synagogue councils should welcome them. In addition, rabbis and cantors ought to be able to serve the spiritual needs of such congregations without feeling ostracized or jeopardizing their careers.

The ordination of gay rabbis is an even more difficult issue. The presumption is that rabbis and cantors are to live their lives according to the ideal of heterosexual marriage and family posited in the Torah. In truth, however, there are gay rabbis and cantors. Many have come out of the closet after ordination; others keep their sexual life a secret from their congregation. Today the Reconstructionist and Reform movements have been willing to ordain homosexuals.

Proponents of ordination acknowledge that the Jewish community can derive great meaning from the personal example of a gay man or woman seeking to live a life of Jewish learning and observance while not denying his or her sexual preference. Such an individual provides a good role model for countless Jews, both gay and straight. Gay Jews who meet the criteria of personal piety, intellect, and commitment to Jewish values ought to be ordained.

Opponents of the ordination of gay Jews claim that rabbis must set the standard for the Jewish community. Can a person be a teacher of Judaism if, even for reasons beyond his or her control, he or she does not live up to the ideal of Judaism? A rabbi who cannot live by the Torah values of marriage, fidelity, and family, according to this view, ought to choose another area of employment.

On this issue I have found much wisdom in Dennis Prager's essay.[27] While expressing compassion for gays, Prager opposes the ordination of individuals who have publicly affirmed their homosexuality. He quotes noted Reform theologian Professor Eugene Borowitz: "To be a rabbi is not a Jewish right but a title bestowed as a special Jewish honor. Rabbis ought to set an example of Jewish ideals."[28]

Prager emphasizes the importance of reaffirming heterosexual marriage as a revolutionary Jewish ideal. He points out that before the Torah, rampant promiscuity, both hetero- and homosexual, was the norm. Judaism's innovation was to advocate that sexuality

> could no longer dominate religion and social life. It was to be sanctified—which in Hebrew means "separated"—from the world and placed in the home, in the bed of husband and wife. Judaism's restricting of sexual behavior was one of the essential elements that enabled society to progress.[29]

Prager opposes any action that undermines the Torah's revolutionary stand about sexuality. His major concern is public advocacy as opposed to private behavior. He compares the case of a gay rabbi to an unmarried rabbi who publicly advocates celibacy as a Jewish ideal. A rabbi can practice celibacy in the privacy of his personal life, but to advocate it publicly is an inappropriate break with Jewish tradition.

Prager writes regarding the ordination of homosexual rabbis:

> Even if . . . it is proven that some people are genetically homosexual, the Jewish principle of exalting marriage and family life would still

have to remain intact. Would this be unfair to the born homosexual who wished to be a rabbi? Yes, it would. But for the sake of society, life is filled with unfairness to individuals. Stutterers, no matter how brilliant, cannot be a radio commentator or talk-show host, because no matter how insightful and witty, they cannot do the job right. The tone-deaf, no matter how deeply they love and understand Beethoven, can never become conductors because they cannot do the job right. Avowed homosexuals, no matter how Jewishly knowledgeable and personally kind, cannot become rabbis because they cannot do the job of being a Jewish role model right.

We live at a time when many people feel that because universal standards can cause pain to some individuals, the standards should be dropped. But the moment a religion or a society has an ideal, some innocent individuals will suffer because of it. The only way to ensure that no individuals feel pain as a result of having standards is to drop all standards. . . .

When a Jewish denomination announces that it has a policy of ordaining practicing homosexuals, it can only mean one of two things: that it considers homosexuality as much a Jewish ideal as heterosexual marriage; or that it does continue to uphold Judaism's marital sexual ideal, but its rabbis no longer need to live by it. It cannot mean anything else.[30]

After much soul searching, I have to agree with Prager. No ordination committee is going to investigate a rabbinic candidate's erotic thoughts or even what occurs in the privacy of his or her bedroom; that is between the candidate and God. Nevertheless, the basic thesis of this book is that the Torah presents a holiness ideal regarding sexual behavior. Even though individual Jews may not live up to that ideal, they have the right to expect their rabbi to exemplify that ideal both in public advocacy and in private behavior. In an age of sexual confusion, Jews can ill afford to take any action that would undermine the Torah ideal.

Equally difficult is the issue of gay marriages. Compassion toward gays is one issue; for society to put a formal stamp of approval upon gay marriage, quite another. According to the midrash, the sin of Egypt and Canaan was actually writing marriage contracts for gay marriages.[31]

The mainstream Jewish community is not ready for official recognition of such marriages. James Nelson, an extremely liberal Christian theologian, writes:

> It is true that the issue of marriage is complicated by the nature of symbolic traditions. As an ordinance or as a sacrament, marriage has a long theological and ecclesiastical history, and that history has been an exclusively heterosexual one. Deeply-rooted symbols are organic. They grow and develop, and sudden changes are seldom successfully legislated.[32]

The Jewish marriage ceremony has a history and a meaning based on the Torah ideal of joining a man and woman under God to build a Jewish home. Traditionally, the rabbi serves as a witness that the ceremony is performed correctly according to Jewish law and the law of the state; the rabbi also represents the Jewish community in blessing the couple. To appropriate the powerful symbols of the Jewish wedding ceremony for a nontraditional union between two people of the same sex would be inappropriate. It would water down the Torah ideal a rabbi is committed to maintain.

Nevertheless, gays as well as heterosexuals seek commitment, community, holiness, and God's blessing in their relationships. Nelson, writing from a Christian perspective, continues his essay:

> Those others who urge the non-celibate gay to seek a permanent relationship, and yet would withhold any liturgical blessing, are saying something . . . insensitive. By withholding full recognition of such sexual covenants the church only, if unintentionally, promotes promiscuity, for it says in effect, "Whatever your relationship is, it is not fit for public Christian affirmation, support, and celebration." To urge a course of action, fully-committed relationships, and then to deny communal and ritual support to those very relationships is to engage in a humanly destructive contradiction.[33]

The same can be said of Jewish relationships. How can the Jewish community ask a gay man or woman to limit sexual activity to a monogamous, loving relationship but not to expect the community officially to approve or bless that relationship?

To solve this dilemma, some rabbis have been willing to perform a "ceremony of commitment" between two people of the same sex. The ceremony is not a Jewish marriage, although it may use some of the symbols and liturgy of a Jewish wedding. Some couples have written and conducted their own ceremony without rabbinic involvement.

Although I understand the need for it, I am not prepared to participate in such a public ceremony. In my view, my role as a rabbi is to represent Jewish tradition and the Torah ideal. I am aware of the powerful personal commitment gay men and women often make to one another, yet I have chosen to confine my rabbinic involvement with gay Jews and their families to the more private realm of counseling.

The role of a counselor is to help individuals make their peace and find self-fulfillment within their situation without being judgmental. The rabbi as counselor should begin where a Jew is and help him or her move toward self acceptance and up the ladder of holiness. Removing guilt is important both for the gay person and his or her family. It is no one's "fault" that someone is gay; parents do not "cause" homosexuality, nor is it "curable" according to most experts. People who are gay need what every human being needs: love, family, a sense of belonging, self-esteem, and acceptance. In these areas rabbis can be extremely helpful.

THE QUESTION OF AIDS

In July 1991 my brother Jeffrey died of AIDS at the age of thirty-seven. He had tested HIV (human immunodeficiency virus) positive about five years earlier and had been ill with full-blown AIDS for about a year and a half. Only a regimen of the powerful drug AZT had delayed the onset of the disease.

At the time of his death, numerous well-meaning people asked me how my brother had contracted AIDS. Was he a hemophiliac? Did he get the disease from a transfusion? The answer is no; my brother was an active gay male during the early eighties when the AIDS epidemic struck. My family knew relatively early that he would eventually die of AIDS; we are thankful that God gave him more years than we originally expected.

The presumption underlying people's questions about my brother is that persons with AIDS are divided into two categories: "innocents" who contracted AIDS through blood transfusions or heterosexual relations, and "non-innocents" who contracted it through shared drug needles and gay sex. By this criterion, my brother was a "noninnocent."

When my brother became ill, he could no longer care for himself, so he moved in with my parents. More than one person questioned them with comments like, "Why take on this burden? After all, he brought this on himself." In the eyes of too many people, my brother and other persons with AIDS deserve their fate.

When my brother finally died, numerous practical issues arose. Jeffrey was not observant, but he wanted to be buried in accordance with Jewish tradition. Sadly, we learned that Jewish burial is not always possible for victims of AIDS. For example, we tried to arrange a traditional *taharah*, the washing of the body as required by Jewish law, but nobody would do it. The question of the role of his gay lover in the funeral also arose.

Underlying all of these problems are some deeper philosophical questions. How do we relate to a disease that so many see as a divine punishment for homosexual behavior? How do we perform the mitzvah of *bikkur ḥolim*, visiting the sick, if the sick person brought the disease on himself or herself? And how do we deal with our own often irrational fear of AIDS?

AIDS is not exclusively a homosexual disease; it can be transmitted by heterosexual as well as homosexual relations with an infected person, by the sharing of needles by drug addicts, and in utero to a baby by an infected mother. Formerly a number of people contracted AIDS through transfusions with infected blood or blood products, but today all blood is screened for the AIDS virus.

In spite of these facts, the public mind associates AIDS with male homosexual activity. The disease was originally identified as the "gay cancer," and even today the majority of victims in America are gay. Many people therefore see AIDS not simply as a disease but as a sign of divine punishment for homosexual activity. In this interpretation, the question of AIDS becomes a religious question.

In many ways, the public reaction to the spread of AIDS is reminiscent of the Bible's treatment of the skin disease *tzara'at*, often mistranslated "leprosy." One who suffered from *tzara'at* was condemned as unclean and turned away from the camp of Israel. (See Lev. 13–14.) The rabbis felt that a person with *tzara'at* was not simply suffering from a disease but had incurred the wrath of God as punishment for a multitude of sins, the most prominent being evil gossip.[34] According to the rabbis, disease (although not necessarily *tzara'at*) was also a consequence of improper sex. To quote the midrash, "Wherever you find sexual license, you may expect disease."[35] As my family learned during my brother's illness, many people still subscribe to the notion that an epidemic such as AIDS is God's punishment for homosexuals, drug abusers, and other "sinners."

In truth, we cannot know the secrets of God. Nobody can authoritatively declare AIDS or any other disease to be a punishment from God. As I said during the eulogy I delivered at my brother's funeral, "AIDS is a disease, not a moral condition."

Rabbi Immanuel Jakobovits, former Chief Rabbi of Great Britain, makes this point powerfully:

> Under no circumstances would we be justified in branding the incidence of the disease, individually or collectively, as punishment that singles out individuals or groups for wrongdoing and lets them suffer as a consequence. We are not inspired enough, prophetic enough, we have not the vision, that would enable us to link, as an assertion of certainty, any form of human travail, grief, bereavement or suffering in general with shortcomings of a moral nature—especially our generation, living as we still do, in the immediate aftermath of the Holocaust.[36]

Ultimately, from our limited, human vantage point, God's reasons are unknowable. Even if AIDS were God's punishment, it would make no practical difference. According to the Talmud, all sufferers from disease deserve our compassion and our commitment to find a cure whether or not their own activity brought about the disease.[37] If we make every effort to cure someone with heart disease or lung cancer, even if his or her eating or smoking habits contributed to the condition, then we owe the same to a person with AIDS.

Our first task is to educate our community about the causes of AIDS and how to prevent it. AIDS is caused by the HIV virus, which is spread through infected bodily fluids, either semen or blood. Sharing needles and having sexual intercourse with an infected person are the main ways the disease is spread. Anal intercourse, because of the bleeding of the tissue, is particularly dangerous, which is why the disease has spread so rapidly within the gay community. By all scientific evidence, AIDS cannot be spread by sharing a swimming pool or a toilet seat or through any other kind of casual contact. AIDS cannot be contracted by donating blood.

Not everybody infected with HIV will necessarily contract AIDS. Some carriers show no symptoms; some show mild symptoms known as ARC (AIDS-related complex). A patient is diagnosed as having AIDS when he or she begins to suffer from certain opportunistic illnesses, most commonly a virulent pneumonia called pneumocystis carinii pneumonia (PCP) or a cancer called Kaposi's sarcoma (KS). Because AIDS destroys the body's defense system, infections that are ordinarily harmless can prove fatal. AIDS patients die not from the virus itself but from the various opportunistic infections that ravish the body. Currently there is no cure for AIDS.

The only protection against AIDS is to avoid the kind of risky behavior most likely to spread the virus: the sharing of drug needles, anal sex with or without a condom, sex with someone who takes drugs intravenously or practices anal sex, sex with prostitutes or anyone whose sexual past is unknown, and sex without a condom with anyone who might be infected. The best protection is either abstinence from sex or sex with a mutually faithful, uninfected partner. Perhaps it is no coincidence that the safest behavior is precisely what both Jewish and Christian tradition teaches: sex belongs in a long-term, mutually faithful, monogamous relationship.

How should Jews react to the AIDS epidemic? First, on an individual level, Jewish tradition says that when disease strikes a person should first scrutinize his or her own behavior. Rabbi Jakobovits makes an important point: AIDS may not be the punishment for a particular behavior, but it is often the consequence.[38] My brother, like most gay men, had no way of knowing the tragic consequences of his behavior, but today the consequences of unprotected promiscuous sex and other types of risky behavior are common knowledge. With an epidemic raging, all human beings should seriously consider whether their own behavior has put themselves and others at risk. Serious self-scrutiny is a legitimate Jewish option; being judgmental toward others is not.

On a community level, the National Jewish Community Relations Advisory Council (NJCRAC) has formulated a national policy on AIDS which opposes mandatory testing because of the fear of discrimination and other more subtle sanctions against those who test positive. NJCRAC's platform also includes legislation to prevent discrimination against persons with AIDS in housing, employment, health care, community services, education, and public accommodation. In addition, it calls for maximum funding for research on the prevention and treatment of AIDS as well as an active public education program.

Unfortunately, the Jewish community tends to deny that such problems as alcoholism, drug abuse, and AIDS affect Jews. There are Jews with AIDS; I have counseled many of them besides my brother. Often they are estranged from synagogue and community life; sometimes they are estranged from their own families. We Jews have a long tradition of care and compassion in the treatment of the ill, which is why the rabbis called the Jewish people *rahamim benai rahamim*—"compassionate children of the compassionate."

Many synagogues and Jewish organizations have developed wonderful projects to help persons with AIDS. Volunteers have been recruited to bring food and run errands for those too sick to help themselves. Persons with AIDS have been invited to Shabbat services, and one synagogue holds a monthly Shabbat dinner for them. Rabbis have done pastoral outreach to AIDS victims, often trying to heal their relationships with other family members. Sensitive rabbis have also recognized that gay persons with AIDS may be involved in a long-term relationship with a sexual partner who may also need support and counseling. When my brother died, his lover said kaddish at the grave side and sat shiva with us. These mourning rituals, I felt, were legitimate because Jewish tradition teaches that people who are not direct relatives but have a significant relationship with the deceased may perform *keriyah* (cut their garment), sit shiva, say kaddish, and participate in other Jewish mourning practices.

AIDS is a disease like any other, but it has struck the gay community with a particular ferocity. For many this fact is an excuse to be less than compassionate, but a judgmental attitude is not the Jewish way. When my brother died, my family and I were so overwhelmed by love and support from the community that we were able to forget the few people who had chosen to blame my brother for his illness.

We Jews must educate our community, particularly our young people, about the causes and prevention of AIDS. We must also fight discrimination against AIDS victims. Finally, we must treat every person with AIDS not as *tzara'at* victims were treated by ancient Israel, but as human beings created in God's image who have been struck by a terrible disease. It takes great love and compassion, but as Jews we can do no less.

9

Raising sexually responsible children

> Mishnah: Do not teach the laws of forbidden sexual relations with three [or more students]. Gemarah: What is the reason? It is logical. When two sit before their teacher, one discusses with the teacher and the other inclines his ear to the instruction. When three sit before their teacher, one discusses with the teacher and the others discuss with each other, miss what their teacher is saying, and may come to permit a forbidden sexual relation. If so, the same should be true for the entire Torah. . . . Forbidden sexual relations are different. They are dear to the soul and the appetite desires them.
>
> *Hagiga 11b*

THIS FASCINATING passage in the Talmud reflects an attitude found in Judaism and in many other classical religious traditions: one should not teach about sex because such teaching may lead to sexual activity. In our own time religious fundamentalists display the same attitude in their unrelenting opposition to sex education in the schools.

Until the previous generation, Jewish parents often held a similar attitude toward sex education. They did not try to teach their children about sex. They attempted to develop decency and modesty in their children, but they spoke of sex only in carefully worded euphemisms when they could not avoid the subject altogether.[1] Jews avoided talking and teaching about sex not only because they were concerned about modesty but because they believed that if they did not talk about sex, their children would not have sex.

In truth, sex education begins long before our children enter school. At a very young age, children learn from their parents' verbal and nonverbal cues certain attitudes toward their body, love, relationships, sexual feelings, and self-esteem. Formal sex education programs in school only build upon attitudes parents have already inculcated in their children. Thus it is parents who bear the primary responsibility for raising sexually responsible children. This duty is part of the parents' mandate to teach a child Torah,[2] for sexual behavior is an essential part of Torah.

The Torah assumes that human beings are sexual creatures. To deny sexuality is to live a life of incompleteness and ill health. Because our bodies, including our sexual drives, are part of God's creation, we ought to cultivate healthy attitudes toward sexuality in our children from a young age. Schools, including Jewish schools, must share some of this responsibility, but the ultimate obligation lies with parents.

Many parents find it difficult to speak with their children about sexuality. Perhaps they have not clarified their own values; perhaps they fear that sex education will force their children to grow up too quickly. Many have difficulty viewing their children as sexual creatures; many grew up in homes in which sex was referred to in vague euphemisms, if at all. Their silence can communicate a powerful message to their children: sexuality is shameful, unhealthy, and an unfortunate necessity of life.

Fortunately, many excellent resources, both secular and Jewish, are available to help parents to raise sexually responsible children. (See the Bibliography.) Ultimately, parents have to trust their own instincts, be honest, and keep the lines of communication open. Sol and Judith Gordon, who have written extensively on this subject, speak of the importance of being an "askable" parent.[3] Too much information, they believe, is better than too little, and it is even acceptable to communicate with a child one's own discomfort with certain topics. Most important, parents must be available and willing to answer questions.

SIX KEYS TO RAISING SEXUALLY RESPONSIBLE CHILDREN

Raising children carries no guarantees, but parents can provide children with six keys that can help them grow into sexually responsible adults: (1) self-esteem, (2) a positive body image, (3) accurate knowledge, (4) Jewish values, (5) a sense of holiness, and (6) proper role models. Each is worthy of some detailed exploration.

Self-Esteem

The Torah contains many passages that demonstrate profound insight into the human personality. The book of Numbers tells of the twelve spies who have just returned from exploring the land of Israel. They first comment on the beauty of the land, saying that "it does indeed flow with milk and honey" (Num. 13:27), but then give vent to their fears, reporting that there are powerful cities and giants in the land; it is unconquerable, they lament. They conclude their report with the verse, "We looked like grasshoppers to ourselves, and so we must have looked to them" (Num. 13:33).

Many commentators have pointed out that if we look like mere grasshoppers in our own eyes, others will see us that way. People who see themselves as meek and vulnerable will be seen by others as easy prey or victims. People who see themselves as unworthy appear unworthy to others. To put it the opposite way, to function successfully in this world, we must begin with self-esteem.

Nowhere is self-esteem more vital than in the area of sexual ethics. In sexual encounters we open the most vulnerable parts of our beings to other people. Significantly, Sol and Judith Gordon begin their book on sex education with a chapter entitled "Promoting Self-Esteem in Children." A person with low self-esteem, they write, feels that he or she deserves poor treatment at the hands of others and that even a poor relationship is better than none. Such low self-esteem can lead to promiscuous sex, premature parenthood, and other self-damaging behavior.[4] On the other hand, young people willing to protect the integrity of their bodies and say "no," whether to offers of drugs, to alcohol, or to premature sex, usually possess a strong self-image.

Developing self-esteem in children is a parent's most important task, one more important than developing book knowledge, artistic talents, or athletic skills in their child. The process begins when parents realize that their child is a unique human being, infinitely valuable and created in the image of God. They never need to put down or mock a child. Even though parents can reprimand or even punish a child for misbehavior, they should convey the notion that the child's behavior, not the child, is bad.

Similarly, children must be praised not only for what they do but for what they are. Rabbi Neil Kurshan writes:

> We must be careful not to give our children the wrong message: that our love is conditional upon their accomplishments. We must love them whether or not they make good grades, go out for extracurricular activities, make the best colleges, take piano and skating lessons.[5]

With these words, Kurshan is merely reformulating the ancient teachings from Pirkei Avot: "Whenever love depends upon some material cause, with the passing away of that cause, the love passes away; but if it be not dependent upon such a cause, it will not pass away forever."[6] In other words, the key to raising children with high self-esteem is to love them unconditionally, to praise them, and to teach them to feel good about themselves.

The Torah teaches the golden rule: "Love your neighbor as

yourself" (Lev. 19:18). Many a commentator has wisely pointed out that people cannot love their neighbors unless they first love themselves. Children whose parents teach them to love themselves will be more likely to grow into an adulthood of loving, caring sexual relationships.

Positive Body Image

Tied to self-esteem is the importance of giving children a positive image of their bodies. Judaism's approach to the body differs radically from that of both classical Christianity and modern secular thought. The former often denigrates the body by subordinating it to the spirit; the latter ignores the spirit, focusing on the body as the only level of reality.

Judaism teaches that both the body and the spirit are God's creations; both are holy, worthy of praise and positive feelings. For this reason Judaism developed the idea of *tehiyat hametim* (bodily resurrection): the rabbis could not imagine the perfect life in the world to come without our physical bodies, for our bodies play a role in God's holiness.

To achieve sexual satisfaction, we must have a positive image of our bodies, but we need not have the bodies of the perfect models that decorate movies and magazine covers. People who are too short or too tall, underweight or overweight; women who have small or large breasts; men who have small or large penises; and people with blemishes or disabilities must also see their bodies as special and holy. Judaism has created a blessing to say upon seeing a person with a body that is in any way unusual: "Praised are You, Lord our God, King of the Universe, who varies the forms of His creatures."

According to Jewish teachings, our bodies do not belong to us but to God. Self-abuse or any other behavior that injures the body is forbidden as an affront to God. A principle in Jewish tort law confirms this teaching:

If one says to another, "blind my eye" or "cut off my hand" or "break my leg," he [who does so] is liable. [Even if he requested him to do so] on condition that he be exempt, he is liable. [If one says to another] "tear my garment" or "break my pitcher," he [who does so] is liable, [If he requested him to do so] on condition he be exempt, he is exempt.[7]

In other words, we can exempt our neighbor from damages to our property but not from damages to our bodies.

Children must be taught from the earliest age not to be ashamed of their bodies. Bodies naturally vary; physical attributes ought to be a source of self-confidence and pride. Even disabilities can be seen as a sign of the variety of God's creation. The Mishnah teaches that God produces many coins from the same stamp, yet each is different.[8]

Children need to learn in a positive way that their bodies can be a source of pleasure. They must feel comfortable with their sense of touch, which raises the issue of masturbation, a question I believe deserves careful rethinking from a Jewish perspective. I deal with the issue of masturbation later in the chapter.

Being comfortable with our bodies does not mean running around naked in front of company. Modesty is also a Jewish virtue that we must inculcate into children. We can teach children that parts of their body are private and should be covered just as we teach them that parts of the body should never be touched or fondled by strangers.

Rabbi Manis Friedman has written on the importance of helping children develop this sense of modesty:

Children are born with an innate sense of modesty. Even certain animals will not mate if they don't have a place to hide. That animals can be modest reveals that modesty is innate in some creatures; it's a fact of nature, and not the product of higher values or noble ideology. In human beings, it's a natural instinct. That's why when a child is abused, what has been violated is the child's inborn modesty. A child who is abused as an infant, even if no violence or pain is incurred, will later show symptoms of abuse.

. . .

The modesty with which all children are born should be strengthened and encouraged, so that as soon as another child or adult makes the slightest attempt at immodesty, the child will know that something is wrong, long before the situation becomes dangerous. Modesty is something children need to know for themselves.[9]

Being comfortable with our bodies means developing self-acceptance, good health habits, the recognition that sexual feelings and pleasure are normal, and self-discipline about the proper context for sexual activity. It means knowing that touching the genitals in the privacy of the bedroom may be appropriate but that doing so in a public place is not. Children who are comfortable with their bodies and treat them with respect have the best chance to grow into adults who treat the bodies of others with dignity and respect.

Accurate Information

Children need facts about sexuality that are appropriate for their age, and parents are the best source of this information. Fortunately, numerous books on the market can also help them. It is better to present too much information to children than too little; they will integrate what they can understand and ignore the rest.

One important rule experts recommend is to use accurate terminology from the beginning. Children will become used to hearing the words "penis," "vagina," and "womb," and accurate terminology transmits the message that sexuality is not shameful and need not be concealed in euphemism. There is no room for vulgarity in a Jewish home when referring to sexual organs or activities.

Children should be taught the basics of biology, including

information about the sexual organs of men and women, how intercourse takes place, and how babies are conceived. As children grow older, they should learn about birth control and sexually transmitted diseases. They should also learn about human sexual response and about the Jewish teaching that sex is one of God's most pleasurable gifts to us.

Children should also be taught to appreciate some degree of modesty and privacy; some subjects like sexuality should be discussed within the privacy of the family rather than in public places. However, parents must let children know that sexuality is part of God's creation and not a cause for embarrassment or anger. Modesty enhances the holiness of sexuality rather than hiding it.

Perhaps most important, as the Gordons suggest, is for adults to become askable parents. Even if they do not know the answers, parents should avoid giving their children the impression that questions about sexuality are off-limits or embarrassing. Parents who discuss sexuality openly with their children when they are young can hope that their children will be comfortable coming to them later if they become sexually active.

Finally, sex education cannot be separated from the Jewish view of sexuality. Judaism regards sex not merely as a biological act but as a significant way in which human beings relate both to one another and to God. In the words of Rabbi Eugene and Estelle Borowitz:

> We do not believe that sex in Judaism can be considered apart from love, from personhood, from the ideal of holiness. To turn sex education into basic biology is to debase it from a Jewish point of view. Biological data are important, but only as a means. The end is a loving human being whose sexuality is expressed with another in a way that makes them both holier—that is, closer to God—than they were before.[10]

In other words, authentic Jewish values are as important as accurate information.

Jewish Values

Reverend Richard John Neuhaus, in a critique of much sex education in this country, writes:

> Indoctrination is a perfectly lovely word that gets a very bad press. Indoctrination is leading people into the doctrine or teachings by which a community desires to live. Yet the word "indoctrination" is piously eschewed by many educators. Education, they say, is not a matter of transmitting teachings but of eliciting the capacity of children to clarify the teachings by which *they* choose to live. In no area is this idea of the child as free agent to be more assiduously respected, such educators insist, than in the area of sexual behavior.[11]

In other words, too often sex education is more values clarification than values transmission.

As I have tried to show throughout this book, Jewish values about sexuality differ radically from both Christian and modern secular values. To teach Jewish values, I gave high school students in a Hebrew high school setting the following eighteen situations and asked them to respond before I shared what I considered the appropriate Jewish response. The subsequent discussion was wonderful!

1. Luann, a high school senior, has a boyfriend who says: "If you love me, you will sleep with me."
2. Jack and Jill decide to live together to see if they are really compatible before marriage.
3. A public high school wants to establish a clinic which will provide birth control for students.
4. Sally is sexually abused by her stepfather, who tells her not to tell anyone.

5. Fred discovers that his wife Sheila has carried on an extramarital affair.
6. Howard and Kate decide to have an open marriage, with permission to seek other sexual partners.
7. Barry decides to remain a virgin until marriage although other boys make fun of him.
8. Janet, fifteen years old, is pregnant after sleeping with her boyfriend.
9. A Jewish high school decides to hold a special sex education class taught by a nurse and a rabbi.
10. Jeff wants his wife Debbie to go to the *mikvah* each month.
11. Steve and Judy tell the rabbi before their wedding that they plan not to have children.
12. A new gay synagogue wants to advertise in the local Jewish newspaper.
13. Rhonda, married with a child, wants to leave her husband for a lesbian lover.
14. George's parents have told him that masturbation is a sin that leads to disease.
15. A pornographic theater opens in a local Jewish neighborhood.
16. Jon likes to brag about his sexual conquests.
17. A youth group is having an overnight trip and wants boys and girls to sleep in the same room.
18. Bob and Laurie, married ten years with no children, decide to have a baby using in vitro fertilization.

The Jewish responses to each of these dilemmas can be found throughout this book. None has a simple solution. From discussions such as these, guided by adults informed about Jewish teachings and sensitive to the concerns of modern young adults, Jewish young people will learn that mature sexuality requires not only ethical responsibility but a pervasive sense of holiness.

A Sense of Holiness

Traditional Jewish observance strives to inculcate in Jews a sense of the holy, of God's presence in day-to-day activities. Part of the job of Jewish parents is to teach their children that sense of holiness. Children who grow up in a home in which the Sabbath day is different and special, certain festivals are set aside for family celebration, prayer and synagogue attendance are a regular part of family life, and eating is an act of discipline proscribing certain foods will begin to understand the Jewish commitment to holiness. Such children will find it far easier than others to apply that sense of holiness to their sexual behavior and to understand how sexuality needs to be sanctified.

Researchers have shown that children who grow up in homes with strong traditional religious values are far less likely to be sexually promiscuous. Some claim that such religious homes are sexually repressive and that children raised in an observant environment develop unhealthy attitudes toward sex characterized by an exaggerated fear of sin. I hope that I have proved in this book that a home can be deeply observant and still have a healthy, open attitude toward sexuality. In fact, children from such homes may have a more mature sexuality because they have developed a sense of holiness about life that carries over into the sexual arena. In addition, children who learn a sense of discipline about what they eat or what they do on the Sabbath will develop the self-discipline to say "no" to promiscuous sexual behavior.

Finally, children who grow up in a home with traditional religious values are likely to mingle with other children who have similar values. Because peer pressure is the strongest force motivating young people to become involved in premature sexual activity, finding peers from families with more traditional values is one way to help young people resist pressure to experiment sexually before they are ready.

I am well aware of the challenge of living an observant life in a secular society. Convincing parents of the importance of inculcating strong ethical values in their children is relatively easy, but giving children that sense of holiness is far more difficult. The Jewish approach to sexuality extends far beyond ethics. It is founded upon the principle that sex is God's gift to humankind to be used with a proper attitude and in a proper context. That attitude grows best in children who are raised with a deep sense of God's presence in the world.

Setting an Example

Ultimately, children learn by example. If sex achieves its highest purpose within the context of a loving relationship, then children who see their parents involved in a loving relationship will develop healthy attitudes toward sex. Children need to see parents who are affectionate toward one another, who touch and kiss and love. They need not see actual sexual intercourse; after all, modesty and privacy are also primary Jewish virtues. What they need most are examples of tenderness and kindness between their parents.

If we want children to grow up faithful to their spouses, they need to see parents who believe in and practice fidelity. If we want children to be comfortable with their bodies, they need parents who are comfortable with theirs. If we want children who do not degrade sex by crude profanity, dirty jokes, or sexist behavior, parents must set the appropriate tone in their household. Above all, they must be consistent; they cannot tell their children that certain language is off-limits and then use it themselves. As a wise writer, whom traditionalists regard as King Solomon, once taught, "Train a lad in the way he ought to go; he will not swerve from it even in old age" (Prov. 22:6).

TEENAGERS AND SEX

Teens are physically ready to have sex long before they are emotionally ready. The rabbis chose thirteen as the age of religious obligation (bar mitzvah) for boys, twelve (bat mitzvah) for girls, because they are the ages at which puberty usually begins for the average child. According to the rabbis, the beginning of sexual maturity marks the beginning of ritual responsibilities.

Teens, however, lack the emotional maturity necessary for a sexual relationship. They usually have neither the self-esteem nor the self-confidence to be truly consenting when confronted with sexual choices. They find it easier to say yes than to say no, particularly when told, "If you really loved me, you would sleep with me." Teens are especially susceptible to powerful peer pressure as well as to pressure from the media. They all too easily confuse lust or physical infatuation with love. In recent years, both boys and girls have often come to view virginity as a source of shame rather than of pride, particularly when they reach the latter teen years and "everyone is doing it."

Often teens are involved in reckless behavior. They feel somehow invulnerable, immune to the dangers inherent in drug use, drinking, fast driving, and irresponsible sex. Because they believe "it can't happen to me," teenagers often become pregnant or contract venereal disease, including AIDS. The emotional storms of the adolescent years often make young people unresponsive to the needs of others.

Too late, teens discover that they are vulnerable, for people who engage in sex open themselves to another person in a very intimate way. An irresponsible sex partner can leave a young person emotionally if not physically scarred. Because of this risk and its serious repercussions, I believe teens are too young to be sexually active.

What should we do when the body is ready but the emotions

are not? The classical answer in Judaism was to arrange for an early marriage. The Talmud teaches, "He who marries off his sons and daughters close to their coming of age is the one of whom it is said, 'And you shall know that your tent is at peace.' "[12] A man was expected to arrange the marriage of his daughter before she became a *bogeret*, an adult woman of twelve and a half. A man could wait longer, until the age of eighteen. Many authorities recommended an even earlier marriage, particularly if a man had lustful thoughts: "R. Hisda said: 'The reason I am brighter than my colleagues is that I married at the age of sixteen; and had I married at fourteen, I would have said to Satan, an arrow in your eye.' "[13]

Today, when education continues until the mid-twenties, such early marriage is obviously not practical. Parents and teachers today have the difficult task of recognizing the sexual pressures on young people and trying to set standards. Parents have a responsibility to communicate to their teenage children that they are not yet ready for sexual intercourse.

Many teens rebel against limits. After all, part of being a teenager is asserting independence by rebelling against parental standards. Nevertheless, young people ultimately respect parents who set standards. Just as it is far easier for a swimmer to kick off from a solid pier than from soft sand, so it is easier to rebel against solid standards than loose, permissive attitudes. In fact, many teens are relieved to be reined in by limits; it gives them an excuse to say no. Telling an aggressive date, "My parents wouldn't approve," is easier than saying, "I'm not ready."

Parents have a responsibility to ensure that their teens do not participate in activities that put inappropriate pressure on them. Parties and youth group retreats should be properly chaperoned. In an overnight retreat or camp, boys and girls should have separate sleeping areas. Young people should have reasonable, age-appropriate curfews. Even if teens are sexually active, parents have a right to set standards for their own home.

If teen sexual activity is to be discouraged, what can teenagers do to relieve the very real sexual tension they feel? With the onset of puberty, the hormones are raging and the sexual drive is immense. The only realistic solution is that perhaps it is time for rabbis to rethink the Jewish prohibition against masturbation.

Traditional Judaism forbids masturbation by males. It has little to say about masturbation by females, although the Talmud does quote a popular folk saying, "He masturbates with a pumpkin and his wife with a cucumber."[14] Many rabbinic sources warn of the evils of "self-abuse."[15] For example, the Talmud teaches, "Rabbi Elazar taught: What is the meaning of the verse, 'Your hands are full of blood'? [Isa. 1:15] This refers to those who pollute themselves with their hands."[16] The classical Hebrew term for masturbation is *hashkhatat zara*, the willful destruction of seed.

Despite the many rabbinic passages about the evil of spilling seed in vain, it is difficult to find a single source for the prohibition in the Torah. The story of Onan (Gen. 38), often cited as the source, involves the more serious biblical sin of evading levirate marriage obligations. Rabbi David Feldman brings a number of possible sources for the law.[17]

The difficulty of pinpointing a biblical source seems to indicate that this is a rabbinic prohibition based on the rabbis' own sense of propriety. As discussed in chapter 6, the prohibition against masturbation is probably based on the mistaken notions that a man has a finite amount of seed, that each seed is a miniature human in potential (homunculus), and that to spill seed is to sap a man's strength. One recent Jewish sourcebook for parents of adolescents calls the sources that denounce masturbation mere "editorial comment":

> While, in Rabbinic, and especially post-Rabbinic literature . . . there is editorial comment denouncing the practice, no punishment is set down. Evidently, it was realized (even then) that the practice was

common and had certain "natural" advantages so that, while it warranted denouncing, the denunciation was (evidently) intended as a control factor to diminish rather than eliminate.[18]

In reality, almost all human beings masturbate at some point in their lives. Mary Calderone and Eric Johnson, experts on sex education, have written that well over 95 percent of males and 75 percent of females masturbate during one or more periods of their lives, often beginning in adolescence and continuing during marriage. They see masturbation as natural and healthy:

> An increasing number of sexologists and sex therapists now agree that masturbation has a specific role to play in the sexual evolution and total life cycle of the human being. They recognize also that great numbers of adults, well into old age, utilize self-stimulation as a form of release and pleasure, sometimes in painful situations such as illness of the partner, or separation by long periods of travel, death, or divorce, but usually as part of ordinary life.
>
> Masturbation can also be looked upon as rehearsal for mature sex. Just as adolescents are constantly trying all sorts of new ways to test their bodies . . . so too they need to find out how their bodies perform sexually. Masturbation is a safe way to do this, because it does not involve another person.[19]

If the overwhelming majority of individuals masturbate, perhaps the rabbinic prohibition belongs to the class of rulings that the rabbis themselves tried to avoid: laws by which the majority of Israel cannot live.[20] If their ruling is based on false information regarding male seed, then it is even more important to rethink the ban on masturbation. Particularly to discourage young people from sexual experimentation with others, we ought to declare forthrightly that masturbation as a form of release, of sexual pleasure, and of learning about the body is permissible.

Of course, in the long run masturbation ought never to be a substitute for an ongoing heterosexual relationship, nor should it be allowed to become an obsession. Masturbation in adults that becomes a substitute for regular sex within marriage or a way of avoiding the obligation of procreation is counter to the Jewish ideal. This point is made clear by one modern Orthodox rabbi, Reuven P. Bulka, in speaking out against masturbation:

> The seed is an instrumentality for conferring love on another. Its being reduced to focus on the self only is considered a heinous crime of the highest order, a moral waste of an opportunity to share and instead using that sharing opportunity selfishly.[21]

Bulka's approach might make sense in a world in which men and women marry shortly after puberty. However, in today's society masturbation ought to be a legitimate alternative for young people not ready for a mature sexual relationship, as well as for adults during various periods of their life when other sexual activity is inappropriate.

Declaring masturbation permissible certainly represents a radical break with tradition, yet it is not without precedent in classical Jewish sources. As we have already shown, Judaism permits the spilling of seed if another legitimate Jewish purpose is served, such as the mitzvah of *onah* (regular sexual fulfillment) for a wife if pregnancy poses a risk for her or for purposes of sperm testing to determine or to enhance fertility. Another source, while not condoning masturbation, sees it as far preferable to other kinds of forbidden sexual practices:

> If a man's inclination is about to overcome him and he fears that he will sin with a married woman, a woman who is a *niddah*, or other forbidden sexual encounter, there are those that say that he can bring forth seed at that point. It is better that he sin with this than with a woman, but afterwards he needs proper atonement.[22]

Even a world which considers masturbation a serious sin regards it as far less serious than adultery or other sexual sins involving other people.

Parents who are extremely uncomfortable with or condemn adolescent masturbation imply to their teenagers that sexual pleasure is dirty and the body is shameful—certainly not a Jewish attitude. Parents ought to be permissive, nonjudgmental, and reasonably casual about teenage masturbation. They should be aware of the multiple sexual stimuli in their teenager's life and urge an appropriate level of privacy and modesty about all sexual matters. To forbid a natural and harmless activity, however, is not only futile but gives young people the wrong impression about sex.

In an ideal world, young people would wait for marriage before they became sexually active. In our less than ideal world, we can hope that young people will wait at least until they are adults involved in mature, loving relationships. The reality, however, is that many young people become sexually active during their teenage years. Parents, teachers, and religious leaders must acknowledge the world as it really is, not as it ought to be.

If they do become sexually active as teenagers, we can hope that young people will have all the tools mentioned above, particularly strong self-esteem, accurate knowledge, and positive moral values. Parents can help them weather these turbulent years by being "askable parents" who listen to their children's questions without anger or intolerance. We do not have to agree with everything our children do to be a loving presence in their lives.

The use of birth control is not as problematic in Judaism as in other religious traditions (see chapter 6). Jewish sources do not mention birth control outside of marriage because of the proscription on nonmarital sex, but it would be irresponsible for any sexually active person not to have protection. It is a parent's responsibility to make sure that sexually active youngsters have access to adequate birth control.

Of course, youngsters do not leap from no sex to full genital intercourse in one step; they move through various levels of sexual experimentation, from rather tentative kissing, to heavy petting with clothes, to genital contact and mutual masturbation. Traditional Judaism forbids all such physical activity between unmarried partners because of fear of the "slippery slope"—that any of these activities will lead to improper sexual intercourse. However, most young people in our society do not and will not abide by a prohibition against all physical contact between members of the opposite sex. Flirting and physical experimentation are part of growing up in today's society.

Recognizing this reality, parents can tell their children that they may draw boundaries within this continuum of physical activity. As we learn in the fourth blessing of the daily Amidah, *hokhmah* (wisdom) is the ability to distinguish boundaries and to abide by them. Thus we can teach our children that kissing is acceptable at a certain age, whereas genital manipulation is not. Parents can help their children set reasonable boundaries for themselves and their partners.

Many young people experiment with homosexual activity as part of growing up. The experimentation grows more out of social circumstances than an affinity to the same sex and is generally not a sign of abnormality or proof that a young person is homosexual. Parents should not overreact to experimental homosexual activity. Most young people, as they grow older, will move on to heterosexual relations. Some, however, will continue to find their erotic fulfillment with members of their own sex. (See chapter 8.)

Unfortunately, in spite of parents' best efforts, teen sexuality often leads to pregnancy. Parents have particular responsibilities in this regard. Punishment and condemnation are not helpful; the pain a pregnant teen experiences is difficult enough. It is important for parents to realize that they have not failed if their daughter becomes pregnant or their son impregnates a young woman; on the contrary, they should take comfort in the fact that their child is able to come to them for advice and help.

Jewish tradition can guide each of the choices faced by a young person dealing with an untimely pregnancy: abortion, adoption, early marriage, or single parenthood. (See chapter 7.) A sympathetic rabbi is an invaluable source of informed, sensitive guidance at such a time. Obviously, the greatest burden falls on the young woman, but a young man also has legal and moral responsibilities. Pregnancy is the most difficult way for young people to learn that sex is more than recreation; it represents a serious responsibility with real obligations.

Above all, parents should let their children know that no matter what happens, they will always be part of a family and will never be rejected. We certainly have a right to set standards and to try to inculcate them into our children, but we should also make clear that our love is absolute, even if our children choose to ignore the standards we set.

10

IMPLICATIONS BEYOND THE BEDROOM

> He has told you, O man, what is good, and what the
> LORD requires of you: Only to do justice and to
> love goodness and to walk modestly with your God.
> *Micah 6:8*

THIS PASSAGE from Micah sums up God's expectations for the Jewish people: to live by justice and mercy, the minimum essentials for ethical behavior; and to walk modestly with God, thereby living a life of holiness. Ethics and holiness are the touchstones of Jewish behavior.

Judaism is a religion of mitzvot, sacred acts that grow out of the relationship between God and the Jewish people. Mitzvot fall into two broad categories: *mitzvot bein adam le-ḥavero* (between a Jew and his or her fellow) and *mitzvot bein adam le-Makom* (between a Jew and God). I prefer to refer to the former as ethical mitzvot and the latter as holiness mitzvot. Both are vital to Jewish life.

The laws that regulate sexual behavior in Judaism encompass both ethical and holiness mitzvot. Sexual ethics thus serve as a powerful paradigm for all of Judaism. Our sexual behavior obviously affects our relationship to our fellow human beings; Judaism teaches that it also affects our relationship to God. Jews are expected to conduct their entire lives, in and out of the bedroom, in a manner that is both ethical and holy.

Judaism lays out both an ethical and a holiness ideal. The ethical ideal is clear: it starts with the mitzvah "Love your neighbor as yourself," and includes the many biblical and rabbinic laws elaborating upon it. Jewish ethics have been well developed in Jewish literature, ranging from rabbinic *aggadot* to medieval moral tracts, and from *musar* literature to hasidic tales. Nevertheless, ethical living, albeit necessary, is not the only requirement of Jewish life; one must also live a holy life.

The holiness ideal is more difficult for modern Jews than the ethical ideal. It starts with the mitzvah "You shall love the Lord your God with all your heart," and includes the many day-to-day activities in which this love is manifested: the cycles of daily prayer, the Sabbath and festivals, the dietary laws, and many of the sexual laws of Judaism. These mitzvot are binding only upon Jews (although other religions articulate their own visions of holiness for their adherents).

Especially in our own time, the holiness ideal is open to different interpretations by the various movements in Jewish life. An Orthodox rabbi's definition of the ideal would sharply differ from that of a Reform rabbi, yet both would agree that our relationship with God must be manifested daily through our actions, and that Jews are not simply an ethical people but "a kingdom of priests and a holy nation."

The paradigm of the ethical and the holy has implications for modern Jews that go beyond the bedroom. It can sharpen our understanding of the meaning of Jewish observance in contemporary Jewish life. On the one hand, partial observance of mitzvot is legitimate in Jewish life. On the other hand, rabbis have a responsibility as spiritual leaders to articulate an ideal in Jewish life.

In chapter 2, I introduced the notion of a ladder of holiness—the idea that Judaism can be described not simply as black and white but in various shades of gray. Thus sexual behavior can be evaluated not simply as moral or immoral, or as good or evil, but as situated on a certain rung on the ladder of holiness. The rabbis established a holiness ideal for sexuality, but few Jews today conduct their lives purely according to that ideal. The hope is that Jews will continually strive for some measure of holiness in their sexual lives, trying to move up the ladder of holiness.

The paradigm of a ladder of holiness provides a model for a Judaism that is not black or white, all or nothing, observant or not observant. It allows for a Judaism beyond the simplistic dichotomies so prevalent in contemporary Israel, where one is either *dati* (religious, observant) or *hiloni* (secular, unobservant). The paradigm requires us to speak in shades of gray and accept the legitimacy of partial observance. Rabbis can encourage their congregants to grow as Jews without demanding an all-or-nothing approach.

The paradigm applies to the kitchen as well as to the bedroom. The holiness ideal mandates what a Jew should eat. A Jew who fully observes the dietary laws according to the classical codes of Jewish law will eat food prepared only in a strictly kosher kitchen or under proper rabbinic supervision. However, what about the Jew who eats dairy foods prepared in a nonkosher kitchen—fish in a restaurant, for example? What about the Jew who keeps a kosher home but eats nonkosher food outside the home? What about the Jew who eats nonkosher meat but avoids mixing it with milk? What about the Jew who mixes milk and meat but avoids pork and shellfish? What about the Jew who does not keep kosher but avoids bread on Passover?

None of these Jews is fully *shomer mitzvot* (observant) in the classical sense. In an all-or-nothing approach to Judaism, each is considered non-observant; there is no sense of any degree of observance. In truth, however, each is observing something; each is somewhere on the ladder of holiness. Some people consider the notion of partial observance illegitimate or even hypocritical. I have heard young people say, "My parents are hypocrites. They keep a kosher home but eat nonkosher out," or, "My parents are hypocrites. They go to synagogue Saturday morning but go shopping Saturday afternoon." Many of these young people use the accusation of hypocrisy to discredit Jewish observance altogether.

The word "hypocrite" is unfair and judgmental. "Inconsistent" is a more accurate term. Most of us are inconsistent about our observance as we move up and down the ladder of holiness; few of us have achieved the holiness ideal. The key for rabbis and other Jewish leaders is to appreciate what Jews *do* observe, not condemn what they do not.

The legitimacy of partial observance was originally endorsed by the extraordinary Jewish thinker and teacher Franz Rosenzweig, who advocated turning the laws of Judaism into commandments. Laws, he argued, are written on paper; commandments are binding on the soul. Rosenzweig was once asked if he put on tefillin each morning as traditional Jewish law demands. He answered, "Not yet." Each of us can indeed legitimately say "not yet" to certain categories of Jewish observance. The hope is that Jews are serious about all areas of Jewish life, including their sexual behavior.

If Jews are to accept the notion of the legitimacy of partial observance, it is particularly vital for rabbis as spiritual leaders to articulate a holiness ideal. What ought to be at the top of the ladder of holiness? Once as I sat on a panel with a social worker and spoke to a large gathering of women on infertility and adoption, someone asked, "What about fertile Jewish couples who decide for personal reasons not to have children?" The social worker spoke first: "Our job is to respect people in whatever life choices they make, not to be judgmental. People have a right to choose to be child-free." I then expressed my disagreement: "Certainly we ought to respect people's decisions, but I am a rabbi, representing a long rabbinic tradition. *Not all decisions are equal.* The ideal is still to 'be fruitful and multiply,' and I have a responsibility to articulate this ideal." Some members of the audience sharply disagreed with me, but most were pleased to see a rabbi stand up for something.

Respecting the integrity of people's decisions is one thing;

saying that all decisions are equal is quite another. Rabbis and other spiritual leaders must articulate an ideal in their preaching, their writing, and their personal lives. A rabbinic counselor thus differs from other therapists, who are by definition nonjudgmental, merely reflecting back the values of their clients.

The rabbi's role in therapy has been clearly articulated by Rabbi Richard Rubenstein:

> There are important differences between religious and psychiatric counseling. . . . The student does not expect non-directive therapy from a clergyman. He comes to a clergyman because the clergyman stands for something. An analyst or a psychiatric counselor need not reveal his own moral commitments in the therapeutic encounter. On the contrary, it is important that the therapist's values become irrelevant in the mind of the client. Such a posture of ethical neutrality is indispensable for therapy. It is impossible and undesirable in religious counseling.[1]

Even if we speak of sexual ethics in shades of gray rather than in black and white, we must not allow our sense of ethics to degenerate into an attitude that all activities and attitudes are equal. In this book I have tried to articulate the Jewish holiness ideal regarding sexual behavior. I am well aware that many, if not most, Jews fail to live up to the ideal, but that fact does not diminish its legitimacy or importance. If nothing else, the ideal serves as an absolute standard by which people can judge their own activity. Rabbis should not only articulate that standard but attempt to live by it in their personal lives.

In this sense, rabbis and spiritual leaders of other faiths play an important role in our secular culture. Holiness is sadly lacking in our materialistic age. A society without a cognizance of the spiritual dimension of life, I fear, will eventually become callous and selfish.

In any quest for spirituality and holiness in society, the government's role is severely limited. It can regulate ethical behavior but in the end has little power to inculcate in its citizens a sense of the holy. Government has a legitimate interest in protecting victims of sexual exploitation; it can outlaw pornography and public nudity. It can even pass laws that are difficult to enforce but have educational value.[2] Laws, however, cannot tell consenting adults how to conduct their sexual lives.

Government does not belong in the bedroom; God does. Ultimately, it is the task of spiritual leaders—rabbis, priests, and ministers—to present moral standards and a vision of holiness for our society. This book is one small attempt to articulate such a vision for modern Jews.

NOTES

Notes to Preface

1. Sanhedrin 6b.
2. Berakhot 45a.

Notes to Chapter 1

1. Berakhot 62a.
2. Seymour J. Cohen, ed. and trans., *The Holy Letter* [attributed to Nahmanides], (New York: Ktav, 1976), p. 42.
3. Eduyot 1:13; Yevamot 62a.
4. Elaine Pagels, *Adam, Eve, and the Serpent* (New York: Random House, 1988), p. 16. This book presents an excellent overview of the identification of sex with original sin in early Christianity.
5. See Sanhedrin 57a.
6. Rashi on Gen. 6:12.
7. See Berakhot 61a.
8. Genesis Rabbah 9:7.
9. Yoma 69a.
10. Sukkah 52a.
11. Sanhedrin 107a.
12. Avot 4:1.
13. Leviticus Rabbah 32:5.
14. Yevamot 6:5.
15. The new Conservative mahzor gives two alternative readings: the traditional one and Leviticus 19, the Holiness Code. See Jules Harlow, ed., *Mahzor for Rosh Hashanah and Yom Kippur*, (New York: The Rabbinical Assembly, 1985), pp. 624, 628.

16. Dennis Prager and Joseph Telushkin, *The Nine Questions People Ask About Judaism* (New York: Simon and Schuster, 1981), p. 78.
17. Berakhot 10a.
18. Avodah Zarah 17a.
19. Yadayim 3:5.
20. Ketubbot 62b.
21. In David Biale, "Eros: Sex and Body," in *Contemporary Jewish Thought*, edited by Arthur A. Cohen and Paul Mendes-Flohr (New York: Charles Scribner's Sons, 1987), p. 179.
22. Sotah 17a.

Notes to Chapter 2

1. Arthur Green, "A Contemporary Approach to Jewish Sexuality," in *The Second Jewish Catalog*, edited by Sharon Strassfeld and Michael Strassfeld (Philadelphia: The Jewish Publication Society, 1976), p. 99.
2. Sanhedrin 56a.
3. Maimonides defines *gilui arayot* more precisely. Six types of illicit intercourse are proscribed to Noahites: a man's mother, his father's wife, his sister on his mother's side, another man's wife (adultery), a male (homosexuality), and an animal (bestiality). *Mishnah Torah*, Hilkhot Melakhim 9:5.
4. See Dennis Prager, "Why I Am a Jew: The Case for a Religious Life," *Ultimate Issues* 2, 2–3 (Spring–Summer 1986): 25–26, on the issue of holiness versus ethics as a guide to sexual behavior.
5. Ibid., p. 24.
6. Joseph Soloveitchik, *Halakhic Man* (Philadelphia: The Jewish Publication Society, 1983), p. 108.
7. For a discussion of the dietary laws as a means of achieving holiness, see Samuel Dresner and Byron Sherwin, *Judaism: The Way of Sanctification* (New York: United Synagogue of America, 1978).
8. Ibid., p. 71.
9. See, for example, John Shelby Spong, *Living in Sin: A Bishop Rethinks Human Sexuality* (San Francisco: Harper and Row, 1988); and James B. Nelson, *Embodiment: An Approach to Sexuality and Christian Theology* (Minneapolis: Augsburg Publishing House, 1978).
10. Jerusalem Talmud 4:12.

11. Quoted in Harold Schulweis, "A Jewish View of Sexuality," *Keeping Posted* 27, 5 (March 1982): 5.
12. Shabbat 30a.
13. Temurot 6:4.
14. See Berakhot 32a; Avodah Zarah 17a; Pesaḥim 113b; Ketubbot 64b.
15. Yevamot 61b.
16. See Gittin 81b.
17. Hasagat Ravad on Rambam, *Mishnah Torah*, Hilkhot Ishut 1:4.
18. Dennis Prager, "Pornography: We Are Asking the Wrong Questions," *Ultimate Issues* (Spring 1988).
19. Ibid., p. 4.
20. Ibid.
21. For a detailed discussion of the laws of modesty, see Louis M. Epstein, *Sex Laws and Customs in Judaism* (New York: Ktav, 1948).
22. Berakhot 24a.
23. Sanhedrin 7a.
24. Robert Gordis, *Love and Sex: A Modern Jewish Perspective* (New York: Women's League for Conservative Judaism, 1978), p. 105.
25. Avot 5:16.

Notes to Chapter 3

1. Sanhedrin 56a.
2. Sol Gordon and Judith Gordon, *Raising a Child Conservatively in a Sexually Permissive World* (New York: Simon and Schuster, 1983).
3. Ibid., p. 41.
4. Sharon Cohen, "Homosexuality and a Jewish Sex Ethic," *Reconstructionist* 56, 8 (July–August 1989): 15–16.
5. Ibid.
6. Rambam, *Mishnah Torah*, Hilkhot Naʿarah Betulah 1:3.
7. Ketubbot 3:4.
8. Rachel Biale, *Women and Jewish Law* (New York: Schocken Books, 1984), p. 241.
9. Ketubbot 51b.
10. Sanhedrin 8:7.
11. Eruvin 100b.
12. Maimonides, *Guide to the Perplexed*, 3:49.

13. Maurice Lamm, *The Jewish Way in Love and Marriage*, (San Francisco: Harper and Row, 1980), p. 42.
14. Sotah 5:1.
15. Rashi on Lev. 19:2.
16. Sotah 9:9.
17. Sotah 47b.
18. Horaot 3:8.
19. *Shulhan Arukh*, Even ha-Ezer 1:14–15.
20. Sanhedrin 71a.
21. Avot 2:5.
22. Lamm, *Jewish Way in Love and Marriage*, p. 43.

Notes to Chapter 4

1. In calling it nonmarital sex instead of premarital sex, I follow the terminology used in Ruth Westheimer and Louis Lieberman, *Sex and Morality: Who Is Teaching Our Sex Standards?* (Boston: Harcourt Brace Jovanovich, 1988); see chap. 5, "Nonmarital Sex: Before and Instead of."
2. Ibid., p. 85.
3. David Feldman, "Sex and Sexuality," in *The Second Jewish Catalog*, edited by Sharon Strassfeld and Michael Strassfeld (Philadelphia: The Jewish Publication Society, 1976), p. 95.
4. Robert Gordis, *Love and Sex: A Modern Jewish Perspective* (New York: Women's League for Conservative Judaism, 1978), p. 170.
5. Eugene B. Borowitz, *Choosing a Sex Ethic*, (New York: Schocken Books, 1969), pp. 113–14.
6. Maurice Lamm, *The Jewish Way in Love and Marriage* (San Francisco: Harper and Row, 1980), p. 31.
7. By rabbinic law, the woman is given the right to refuse to marry, or once married, to demand a divorce. See Rambam, *Mishnah Torah*, Hilkhot Na'arah Betulah 1:3.
8. Ketubbot 1:2.
9. See Ketubbot 1:5.
10. Sanhedrin 75a.
11. Technically, a man was permitted to arrange the marriage of his daughter while she was still a minor. However, the rabbis dis-

couraged this until the girl was old enough to give her consent. See Kiddushin 41a.

12. Kiddushin 29b–30a.

13. Kiddushin 1:1.

14. Kiddushin 12b.

15. Gittin 81b.

16. The scope of this ruling was later severely limited. If every couple who has sexual relations is presumed to have marital intent, a *get* (Jewish divorce) would then become obligatory. To prevent this problem, the rabbis limited the ruling to divorced couples who are seen cohabiting with one another. There are different opinions regarding the marital status of a couple who has lived together many years in a marriagelike relationship.

17. Louis M. Epstein, *Sex Laws and Customs in Judaism* (New York: Ktav, 1948), p. 11.

18. Tosefta Kiddushin 1.

19. Sanhedrin 21a.

20. Rambam, *Mishnah Torah*, Hilkhot Ishut 1:1–4.

21. *Hassagat ravad* on Rambam, Hilkhot Ishut 1:4.

22. Sanhedrin 21a.

23. Jacob Emden, *She-elat Yabetz*, pt. 2, no. 15.

24. The principle is based on a rabbinic reading of the verse from Psalms, "It is time to act for the LORD, for they have violated Your teaching" (Ps. 119:126); see Temurah 14b.

25. Yevamot 62b.

26. Yeroham Tsuriel, "The Kedushah of Monogamy: A Personal Perspective," in *Jewish Marital Status*, edited by Carol Diament (Northvale, N.J.: Jason Aronson Inc., 1989), p. 64.

27. Sifra Kiddushin 7:5.

28. See Robert Gordis, "A Proposal for the Text of the Ketubbah," in *Proceedings of the Committee on Jewish Law and Standards of the Conservative Movement* (New York: The Rabbinical Assembly, 1988), p. 200.

29. Ibid.

30. See Morris M. Shapiro, "The Text of the Ketubbah," in *Proceedings*, p. 193.

31. Kiddushin 40a.

Notes to Chapter 5

1. Yevamot 62b.
2. Kiddushin 19b.
3. This section is an expansion of Michael Gold, "God in the Bedroom," *Moment* 16, 4 (August 1991): 37–41.
4. David Feldman, *Marital Relations, Birth Control, and Abortion in Jewish Law* (New York: Schocken Books, 1978), p. 61.
5. Ketubbot 5:6.
6. Pesaḥim 72b.
7. Ketubbot 62b.
8. Pesaḥim 72b.
9. Naḥmanides, *The Holy Letter* (*Iggeret ha-Kodesh*), translated and edited by Seymour J. Cohen (New York: Ktav, 1976), pp. 140–44.
10. Niddah 71a.
11. Niddah 31a.
12. Shabbat 140b.
13. Rashi to Shabbat 140b, d.h. nakit.
14. Eruvin 100b.
15. Ketubbot 5:7.
16. Ketubbot 64b. For a fuller treatment of the law of the rebellious wife, see Shlomo Riskin, *Women and Jewish Divorce* (Hoboken, N.J.: Ktav, 1989).
17. Ketubbot 63b.
18. Eruvin 100b.
19. Ketubbot 48a.
20. *Shulḥan Arukh*, Even ha-Ezer 76:13. I thank Rabbi Reuven Bulka for pointing out this source to me.
21. Berakhot 22a.
22. Niddah 17a.
23. Rambam, *Mishnah Torah*, Hilkhot Issurei Biah 21:10.
24. Niddah 17a.
25. Meiri to Niddah 17a.
26. Gittin 70a.
27. Nedarim 20b.
28. Rambam, *Mishnah Torah*, Hilkhot Issurei Biah 21:9.
29. Rashi on Yevamot 34b, d.h. shelo.
30. Tosefot to Yevamot 34b, d.h. velo.

31. Nedarim 20b.
32. Ibid.
33. Sanhedrin 7a.
34. This section is an expansion of Michael Gold, "Family Purity—A Fresh Look at the Mikvah," *Moment* 14, 2 (March 1989): 32–35.
35. Niddah 31b.
36. Niddah 66a.
37. For a fuller treatment of this issue, see Michael Gold, *And Hannah Wept: Infertility, Adoption, and the Jewish Couple* (Philadelphia: The Jewish Publication Society, 1988), pp. 94–100.
38. Shabbat 2:6.
39. Elyse M. Goldstein, "Take Back the Waters: A Feminist Re-Appropriation of Mikvah," *Lilith*, no. 15 (Summer 1986): 16.
40. Blu Greenberg, *On Women and Judaism* (Philadelphia: The Jewish Publication Society, 1981), p. 121.
41. David C. Kraemer, "A Developmental Perspective on the Laws of Niddah," *Conservative Judaism* 38, 3 (Spring 1986): 30–31.

Notes to Chapter 6

1. This material receives a fuller treatment in Michael Gold, *And Hannah Wept: Infertility, Adoption, and the Jewish Couple* (Philadelphia: The Jewish Publication Society, 1988), pp. 18–28.
2. Nedarim 64b.
3. Yevamot 6:6.
4. Yevamot 65b.
5. Kiddushin 2b.
6. For example, see Rashi on Gen. 3:16.
7. Meshekh Hokhmah to Gen. 9:7, quoted by David S. Shapiro in *Jewish Bioethics*, edited by F. Rosner and J. D. Bleich (New York: Sanhedrin Press, 1979), p. 65.
8. Yevamot 65b.
9. Avot 5:25.
10. Kiddushin 29b.
11. See also Rashi on Gen. 4:19.
12. Yevamot 62b.
13. Yevamot 63b.

14. Sotah 12a.
15. Berakhot 10a.
16. For a more complete overview of the Jewish approach to birth control and related issues, see David M. Feldman, *Marital Relations, Birth Control, and Abortion in Jewish Law* (New York: Schocken Books, 1978).
17. Yevamot 12b.
18. Tosefot on Yevamot 12b, d.h. shalosh.
19. Yam Shel Shlomo, Yevamot 1:8.
20. Yevamot 65b.
21. Tosefta Yevamot 8:2.
22. Moshe David Tendler, *Pardes Rimonim* (New York: The Judaica Press, 1979), p. 17.
23. For a number of such sources, see Alex Goldman, *Judaism Confronts Contemporary Issues* (New York: Shengold Publishers, 1978), pp. 126–34.
24. Tosefot on Shabbat 110b, d.h. vehatanya.
25. For a full treatment on this subject, see Feldman, *Marital Relations*, pp. 235–44.
26. See Rashi on this passage.
27. Niddah 13b.
28. Zohar, Vayeshev 188a, quoted in Feldman, *Marital Relations*, p. 115.
29. Niddah 13b.
30. See Gold, *And Hannah Wept*, pp. 88–94.
31. Yevamot 34b.
32. Mary S. Calderone and Eric W. Johnson, *The Family Book about Sexuality* (New York: Harper and Row, 1989), p. 158.
33. Yevamot 75b.
34. Walter Jacob, *Contemporary American Reform Responsa* (New York: Central Conference of American Rabbis, 1987), p. 293.
35. See Gold, *And Hannah Wept*, for a further study of adoption as a Jewish option.
36. "Understanding AIDS: A Message from the Surgeon General" (Washington: U.S. Department of Health and Human Services, 1988), p. 4.
37. Immanuel Jakobovits, "Halachic Perspectives on AIDS," *Jewish Press*, Aug. 16, 1991, p. 22B.
38. Hullin 10a.

39. See "Instruction on Respect for Human Life in Its Origin and on the Dignity of Procreation," *Origins* 16, 40 (March 19, 1987): 708.
40. For a detailed discussion, see Gold, *And Hannah Wept*, chap. 5.
41. For a further discussion of the importance of bloodlines and Judaism, see Michael Gold, "Adoption: A New Problem for Jewish Law," *Judaism* 36, 4 (Fall 1987): 443–50.
42. Sanhedrin 19b.

Notes to Chapter 7

1. For one example of a nonreligious Jew who uses a biological argument to oppose abortion, see Bernard Nathanson, *Aborting America* (New York: Pinnacle Books, 1981).
2. Hullin 58a.
3. Sotah 30b.
4. Sanhedrin 4:1.
5. David M. Feldman, *Marital Relations, Birth Control, and Abortion in Jewish Law* (New York: Schocken Books, 1974), p. 282.
6. Oholot 7:6.
7. Rashi on Sanhedrin 72b.
8. Rambam, *Mishnah Torah*, Hilkhot Rotzeah u-Shemirot ha-Nefesh 1:9.
9. Arakhin 7a.
10. She-elat Ya'avetz, no. 43, quoted in Feldman, *Marital Relations*, p. 288.
11. Resp. Or Gadol, no. 31, in ibid., p. 287.
12. Yevamot 69a.
13. Sanhedrin 57b.
14. Tosefot on Sanhedrin 59a, d.h. lecha.
15. Ronald Dworkin, "The Great Abortion Case," *New York Review of Books* 36, 11 (June 29, 1989): 52.
16. Yoma 83a.
17. Immanuel Jakobovits, *Jewish Medical Ethics* (New York: Bloch Publishing Co., 1959), pp. 180–81.
18. Mary Ann Glendon, *Abortion and Divorce in Western Law* (Cambridge: Harvard University Press, 1987), p. 46.
19. Ibid., p. 15.
20. Ibid., p. 59.
21. Hullin 9b.
22. Carl Alpert, "Report from Israel," *The Jewish Week* (October 25–31,

1991): 19. For more information, contact Just One Life, 1 East 33rd St., Suite 700, New York, NY 10016.

Notes to Chapter 8

1. Walter S. Wurzburger, "Preferences Are Not Practices" *Judaism* 32 (Fall 1983): 425.
2. Sefer haHinukh, no. 209.
3. Rabbi Baruch haLevi Epstein, *Torah Temimah* on Lev. 18:22.
4. Nedarim 51a.
5. Reuven P. Bulka, *The Jewish Pleasure Principle* (New York: Human Sciences Press (1987), p. 107.
6. Kiddushin 4:14.
7. Kiddushin 82a.
8. *Shulhan Arukh*, Even ha-Ezer 24, Bayit Hadash to Tur on this passage.
9. David M. Feldman, "Homosexuality and Jewish Law," *Judaism* 32 (Fall 1983): 427.
10. Yevamot 76a.
11. Rambam, *Mishnah Torah*, Hilkhot Issurei Biah 21:8.
12. Norman Lamm, "Judaism and the Modern Attitude to Homosexuality," *Encyclopedia Judaica Yearbook 1974* (Jerusalem: Keter Publishing House, 1974), p. 203.
13. Feldman, "Homosexuality and Jewish Law," p. 429.
14. Hershel J. Matt, "A Call for Compassion," *Judaism* 32 (Fall 1983): 430–31.
15. Ibid., p. 432.
16. Janet Marder, "Jewish and Gay," *Keeping Posted* 32, 2 (November 1986): 7.
17. James B. Nelson, *Embodiment: An Approach to Sexuality and Christian Theology* (Minneapolis: Augsburg Publishing House, 1978), p. 198.
18. Judith Plaskow, *Standing Again at Sinai: Judaism from a Feminist Perspective* (San Francisco: Harper and Row, 1990), pp. 208–9.
19. Robert Kirschner, "Halakhah and Homosexuality: A Reappraisal," *Judaism* 37 (Fall 1988): 450–58.
20. Ibid., p. 453.
21. Ibid., p. 457.
22. Ibid., p. 458.

23. Quoted in Janet Marder, "Our Invisible Rabbis," *Reform Judaism* 19, 2 (Winter 1990): 6.

24. Christie Balka and Andy Rose, eds., *Twice Blessed* (Boston: Beacon Press, 1989).

25. Martin Bauml Duberman, "Twice Blessed or Doubly Other?" review of *Twice Blessed*, edited by Christie Balka and Andy Rose, *Tikkun* 5 (March–April 1990): 104.

26. Lamm, "Judaism and the Modern Attitude to Homosexuality," p. 204.

27. Dennis Prager, "Judaism, Homosexuality, and Civilization," *Ultimate Issues* (April–June 1990).

28. *New York Times*, June 27, 1989, quoted in Prager, "Judaism, Homosexuality, and Civilization," p. 19.

29. Ibid., p. 3.

30. Ibid., pp. 20–21.

31. Sifra 9:8.

32. Nelson, *Embodiment*, p. 208.

33. Ibid. pp. 208–9.

34. Tosefta Negaim 6:7; Arakhin 15b.

35. Jerusalem Talmud, Sotah 1:5.

36. Immanuel Jakobovits, "Halachic Perspectives on AIDS," *The Jewish Press*, August 9, 1991, p. 38.

37. Sotah 32b.

38. Jakobovits, "Halachic Perspectives on AIDS."

Notes to Chapter 9

1. See Estelle Borowitz and Eugene B. Borowitz, "Talking with Our Children about Sex," in *The Jewish Family Book*, edited by Sharon Strassfeld and Kathy Green (New York: Bantam Books, 1981).

2. Kiddushin 29a.

3. Sol Gordon and Judith Gordon, *Raising a Child Conservatively in a Sexually Permissive World* (New York: Simon and Schuster, 1983), chap. 4.

4. Ibid., pp. 26–27.

5. Neil Kurshan, *Raising Your Child to Be a Mensch* (New York: Atheneum, 1987), p. 50.

6. Avot 5:19.

7. Bava Kamma 8:7. I thank Rabbi Sol Roth for his insight into this Mishnah.

8. Sanhedrin 37a.

9. Manis Friedman, *Doesn't Anyone Blush Anymore? Reclaiming Intimacy, Modesty and Sexuality* (San Francisco: Harper and Row, 1990), pp. 93, 97.

10. Borowitz and Borowitz, "Talking with Our Children about Sex," p. 241.

11. Richard John Neuhaus, "Church Teaching on Sexuality: From St. Paul to Rod McKuen," *Orange County Register*, August 8, 1988.

12. Yevamot 62b.

13. Kiddushin 29b.

14. Megillah 12a,b.

15. For a full talmudic discussion, see Niddah 13a, 13b.

16. Niddah 13b.

17. David Feldman, *Marital Relations, Birth Control, and Abortion in Jewish Law* (New York: Schocken Books, 1974), chap. 6.

18. *Parent Education for Parents of Adolescents: Teacher's Manual*, Family Education Committee, United Synagogue Commission on Jewish Education (1981), p. 48.

19. Mary Calderone and Eric Johnson, *The Family Book about Sexuality* (New York: Harper and Row, 1989), p. 25.

20. Avodah Zarah 36a.

21. Reuven P. Bulka, *The Jewish Pleasure Principle* (New York: Human Sciences Press, 1987), p. 109.

22. Encyclopedia Talmudit, quoted in *Assia* 11, 4 (April 1988): 41. The original source is *Sefer Hasidim* 176 (my translation).

Notes to Chapter 10

1. Richard L. Rubenstein, "The New Morality and College Religious Counseling," in *Rabbinical Counseling*, edited by Earl Grollman (New York: Bloch Publishing Co., 1966), pp. 26–27.

2. For a study of the educational value of law, see Mary Ann Glendon, *Abortion and Divorce in Western Law* (Cambridge: Harvard University Press, 1987).

GLOSSARY

Betultah   Aramaic word for virgin, used in marriage *ketubbah*.

Biyah ke-darkah   Natural sex.

Biyah lo ke-darkah   Unnatural sex.

Ervah   Sexually suggestive; nakedness.

Gemarah   Discussions of the Mishnah collected around 500 CE. The Mishnah and the Gemarah together make up the Talmud.

Gilui arayot   Literally, "uncovering nakedness"; the term refers to forbidden sexual activities.

Halakhah   Jewish law.

Hashkhatat zara   Forbidden spilling of seed.

Het   Sin; literally, "missing the mark."

Hol   Secular, profane; the opposite of *kodesh*.

Kadosh   Holy.

Ketubbah   The traditional marriage document; also a sum of money the husband or his estate is obligated to pay the wife in the event of divorce or death.

Kiddushin   Marriage.

Kodesh   Holiness; the opposite of *hol*.

Kohen   Priest, a descendant of Aaron.

Levi   A descendant of the tribe of Levi, a tribe given special religious status.

Mamzer   A Jew born of an adulterous or incestuous relationship.

Mikvah   A ritual bath.

Mishkav zakhar   Male homosexual sex.

Mishnah   The collection of oral law from 200 CE that forms the core of the Talmud.

Mitzvah   A commandment.

Mokh   An absorbent tampon used by woman as a birth control device.

Moredet   A wife who refuses to have sex with her husband.

Nafal   A miscarriage or aborted fetus; also a baby who dies before the age of thirty days.

Niddah   A woman during her menstrual cycle.

Onah   A man's duty to have regular sexual relations with his wife.

Ones   Being forced against one's will.

Pidyon ha-ben   Redemption of first born son.

Rodef   A pursuer with intent to kill, injure, or rape.

Shalom bayit   Peace in the house.

Simhat ishto   The law stating that a man should make his wife happy with the sexual act.

Sotah   A woman suspected by her husband of adultery, who must go through a trial by ordeal.

Taharat ha-mishpahah   Family purity; a euphemism for the laws of niddah and mikvah.

Tahor   Ritually pure.

Tamei   Ritually impure.

Teshuvah   Return to the correct path; return to God.

To'evah   Abomination.

Tzara'at   A skin disease, often translated as leprosy.

Tzniyut   Modesty.

Ubar   A fetus in the womb.

Yetzer hara   The evil inclination, often identified with the sex drive.

Yetzer hatov   The good inclination.

Yihud   A man and a woman alone together.

Zenut   Promiscuity; prostitution.

Zonah   A prostitute.

BIBLIOGRAPHY

The following English language books are recommended to readers for further study.

General Sources

Biale, Rachel. *Women and Jewish Law*. New York: Schocken Books, 1984.

Bulka, Reuven P. *The Jewish Pleasure Principle*. New York: Human Sciences Press, 1987.

Epstein, Louis M. *Sex Laws and Customs in Judaism*. New York: Ktav, 1948.

Feldman, David. *Marital Relations, Birth Control, and Abortion in Jewish Law*. New York: Schocken Books, 1974.

Westheimer, Ruth, and Louis Lieberman. *Sex and Morality: Who Is Teaching Our Sex Standards?* Boston: Harcourt Brace Jovanovich, 1988.

Christian Sources

Nelson, James. *Between Two Gardens*. New York: Pilgrim Press, 1983.

———. *Embodiment: An Approach to Sexuality and Christian Theology*. Minneapolis: Augsburg Publishing House, 1978.

Pagels, Elaine. *Adam, Eve, and the Serpent*. New York: Random House, 1988.

Spong, John Shelby. *Living in Sin: A Bishop Rethinks Human Sexuality*. San Francisco: Harper & Row, 1988.

Sources on Nonmarital Sex

Borowitz, Eugene. *Choosing a Sex Ethic*. New York: Schocken Books, 1969.

201

Gordis, Robert, *Love and Sex: A Modern Jewish Perspective*. New York: Women's League for Conservative Judaism, 1978.

Sources on Marital Sex and Family Purity

Cohen, Seymour, ed. and trans. *The Holy Letter*. New York: Ktav, 1976.

Kaplan, Aryeh. *Waters of Eden*. New York: Jewish Pride and Identity, 1984.

Lamm, Maurice. *The Jewish Way in Love and Marriage*. San Francisco: Harper and Row, 1980.

Lamm, Norman. *A Hedge of Roses*. New York: Philip Feldheim, 1966.

Sources on New Reproductive Techniques and Abortion

Glendon, Mary Ann. *Abortion and Divorce in Western Law*. Cambridge: Harvard University Press, 1987.

Gold, Michael. *And Hannah Wept: Infertility, Adoption, and the Jewish Couple*. Philadelphia: The Jewish Publication Society, 1988.

Sources on Homosexuality

Balka, Christie, and Andy Rose, eds. *Twice Blessed*. Boston: Beacon Press, 1989.

Boswell, John. *Christianity, Social Tolerance, and Homosexuality*. Chicago: University of Chicago, 1980.

Sources on Sex Education

Calderone, Mary S., and Eric W. Johnson. *The Family Book about Sexuality*. New York: Harper and Row, 1989.

Friedman, Manis. *Doesn't Anyone Blush Anymore?* San Francisco: Harper and Row, 1990.

Gordon, Sol, and Judith Gordon. *Raising a Child Conservatively in a Sexually Permissive World*. New York: Simon and Schuster, 1983.

Kurshan, Neil. *Raising Your Child to Be a Mensch*. New York: Atheneum, 1987.

INDEX

Make books your companion
Let your bookshelf be your garden—
Judah Ibn Tibbon

to become a member –
to present a gift –

call 1 (800) 234-3151
or write:
The Jewish Publication Society
1930 Chestnut Street
Philadelphia, Pennsylvania 19103

A Jewish Tradition